MORE
CLASSIC OLD HOUSE PLANS

AUTHENTIC DESIGNS FOR COLONIAL AND VICTORIAN HOMES

MORE CLASSIC OLD HOUSE PLANS

Authentic Designs for Colonial & Victorian Homes

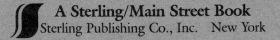
A Sterling/Main Street Book
Sterling Publishing Co., Inc. New York

Lawrence Grow

Library of Congress Cataloging-in-Publication Data

Grow, Lawrence.
   More classic old house plans.

   Bibliography: p.
   1. Architecture, Domestic—United States—Designs
and plans.   2. Architecture, Colonial—United States—
Designs and plans.   3. Architecture, Victorian—United
States—Designs and plans.   I. Title.
NA7205.G769   1986   728.3′7′0223   86-8441
ISBN 0-915590-86-7

Designed by Lisa Magaz

10 9 8 7 6 5 4 3 2 1

A Sterling / Main Street Book

© 1986 by The Main Street Press
Published by Sterling Publishing Company, Inc.
387 Park Avenue South, New York, N.Y. 10016
Distributed in Canada by Sterling Publishing
℅ Canadian Manda Group, P.O. Box 920, Station U
Toronto, Ontario, Canada M8Z 5P9
Distributed in Great Britain and Europe by Cassell PLC
Artillery House, Artillery Row, London SW1P 1RT, England
Distributed in Australia by Capricorn Ltd.
P.O. Box 665, Lane Cove, NSW 2066
Manufactured in the United States of America
All rights reserved

ISBN 0-915590-86-7

CONTENTS

Introduction

By studying authentic house plans from the past, it is possible to avoid many mistakes made in restoring or remodeling an old house or in building a new "old" house. When driving around the countryside during these days of intense building activity, the temptation is always great to leap from the car and to yell halt when spotting yet another architectural atrocity in the works. The saltbox with scalloped aluminum storm doors is a minor nuisance; the stone Georgian Colonial about to receive a modern bay window makes the blood boil; but the ultimate insult is to see the application of a high-style feature such as a Georgian broken pediment over the entrance to a simply framed Greek Revival house or a gingerbread Victorian cottage. It is not the mixing of styles which offends, but the mixing of the *wrong* styles. Materials and lines must blend together; proper proportions have to be maintained; there should be some sort of stylistic affinity between one element and another.

The same rules apply, of course, to the building of a new home in a period style. Too often, the new homeowner follows plans ripped out of a lumberyard brochure or a cheap builder's magazine. The Cape Cod with a wrought-iron front porch railing, two-car garage facing the street, and a gargantuan cupola and weathervane is one of the most popular horrors now circulating in house plan form.

Nearly everyone has a house of his dreams. Something similar may be found in these pages filled with real, not imaginary, historic buildings. All of the houses, however, will require alteration or adaptation to meet individual needs. In almost every case, these are homes which have already gone through some period of change, possibly acquiring different but complementary stylistic elements, and survived to tell the tale. Through a careful study of the floor plans, elevations, and details, the essential lines and proportions and the correct materials will emerge.

The plans in *More Classic Old House Plans* are drawn from the archives of the Historic American Buildings Survey housed in the Library of Congress, Washington, D.C. The buildings date from the mid-1600s to the early 1900s. Most are modest, small-scale dwellings of five or six rooms, the size home in which the average family lived then and lives today. Only the later designs include such modern improvements as indoor plumbing and a central heating system, but these necessities can be incorporated in any of the plans by an understanding architect or home builder without destroying the building's lines. More importantly, the drawings and floor plans provide the essential details which illustrate and explain the workings of a period house and its true historic character.

Houses are grouped simply as Colonial or Victorian, and within these categories, by three sections—early, mid-, and late. Whenever possible, clear distinctions are drawn between various types of Colonial and Victorian architecture, such as Georgian or Greek Revival or Queen Anne, etc. The majority of the houses, however, do not fit into neat classifications since they partake of elements from various periods. The houses have changed with time in a generally harmonious fashion. For the most part, these are vernacular houses, of which America has an abundance. Great houses are usually the only buildings which are stylistically perfect for they were the only ones to have been based on the designs of a knowledgeable, fashionable architect of the time. Such houses can provide many lessons in architectural style, but their plans are often difficult to translate in practical terms.

Colonial Home Plans

Early Colonial

The earliest permanent homes built in the English colonies of North America were—of necessity—small in size, extremely simple in decoration, and uncomplicated in layout. The houses were usually of frame construction as timber for lumber was available virtually everywhere. Timbers, simply hewn, were also used for structural purposes, and in the case of the log cabin served as the primary building material. If other building materials such as fieldstone, quarried cut stone, or clay to make bricks could be easily obtained, one or a combination of these might be used in place of wood. If in short supply, brick or stone might be reserved for such uses as chimneys, hearths, and foundations.

Although there was no uniform building code to follow or even pattern books to consult in the 17th century, people of the same cultural background tended to build similar types of houses and to site them in similar ways. Studies of early New England domestic architecture indicate that differences in style are in part a result of varying English regional building traditions. A colonist from East Anglia, for example, might build a somewhat different house than a settler from the West Country. By the early 18th century, however, these regional differences were beginning to disappear among colonists of English origin everywhere.

One of the most common early Colonial building types found on the East Coast is the two-room-wide, one-room-deep building. It might have begun life as a single-room dwelling. The size varies, but few of these buildings are more than 30 feet long by 20 feet wide. In height, the houses range from a single story with attic space to two-and-a-half stories. In New England houses, the chimney is usually centered and provides fireplaces for the two principal rooms. Architectural historians refer to the common layout as a "hall/parlor" arrangement. What would now be considered a front hall is a small entry area situated alongside the massive chimney. The hall proper on one side of the house is a larger space and served as the kitchen and dining area. A parlor on the other side of the house is a living room and might also contain a bed or beds. A New England house of this type was most often expanded with the addition of a shed extension at the rear, thus creating the "salt-box" form. A new kitchen was usually situated in the rear.

Similar houses exist in the Middle Atlantic and Southern states. In the former region, stone was used much more often than in New England; brick was also more common here as well as in the South. A chimney was often built into each gable end of these houses rather than in the center. This is found to be true in houses built by English as well as Dutch, German, and Swedish settlers. In the earliest houses, narrow stairs ascend the side of the chimney and are aptly named tightwinders or closet stairs.

The early Dutch houses of New York, New Jersey, and Delaware are usually distinguished by the flaring eaves of the roof line. This feature is clearly seen in the Samuel Demarest House (pp. 16-19). Other unusual features are the so-called double Dutch doors and a front stoop sheltered by the overhanging eave.

Many of the patterned brickwork houses of South Jersey, Maryland, and northern Virginia originally had a two-room hall/parlor floor plan. These buildings are the most decorative and the largest in scale of the early Colonial dwellings. Elaborate brickwork decoration was primarily used for houses in the early 1700s after the first generation of settlers was well established. The Denn House (pp. 28-29) is typical of this kind of building.

All of the houses shown in this section are essentially pre-Georgian. Some have had "improvements" over time which have given them a more symmetrical, formal appearance in keeping with the Georgian style. But they remain in basic layout and composition without substantial decorative embellishment. Each simple structure defines itself without the addition of elaborate moldings, pediments, and columns.

1. **Governor Thomas Prence House**, Eastham, Massachusetts, 1646. The Prence house, not unduly modest for the residence of an elected official of the time, had fallen to ruin as early as the 1930s when these drawings were completed. Measurements of the cellar and descriptions of the building by elderly residents of the Cape Cod community enabled the elevations and floor plan to be reconstructed. Many details, however, are conjectural. What was being recalled by inhabitants born in the mid-1800s was, of course, not the original building but a later version. The first windows used in the 1600s might have been smaller and casement rather than sash. The entrance has obviously changed and the original door was probably vertical board and batten.

The off-center chimney stack is an unusual feature as is the two-deep room arrangement. The original room layout may have been somewhat closer to the typical two-room hall/parlor arrangement, the hall occupying the area now designated the kitchen. The parlor would have occupied all the remaining space. The dimensions, 25′ x 29′3″, are by no means spacious, but they were more than adequate for an early New England family. The second-floor layout has not been reconstructed, but it surely included at least two bedrooms.

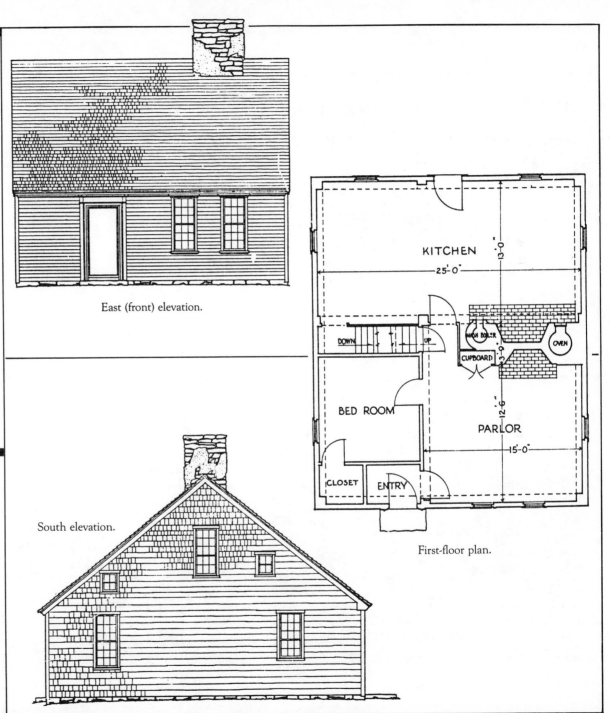

East (front) elevation.

South elevation.

KITCHEN

BED ROOM

PARLOR

CLOSET   ENTRY

First-floor plan.

South (front) elevation.

West elevation.

2. **George Blanchard House**, Medford, Massachusetts, 1657-58. A true center-hall Colonial with a salt-box profile, the Blanchard residence is distinguished by its gambrel roof and shed addition. There is some question regarding the date of completion of the main portion, some historians claiming a time closer to the turn of the 17th century. There is no question, however, that the rear extension came later, thus enlarging the house from a two-room wide, one-room deep layout to a depth of two rooms. Dotted lines in the first-floor plan indicate that there was a fireplace and oven in the present dining room and that the room once served as the kitchen. The porch, entrance, and sash windows are also unquestionably later additions. Pins in the wall beams of the first-floor front section suggest that there were uprights that framed in casement windows.

The gable ends and rear façade are shingled, approximately 6″ to weather. The front is clapboard-sided, about 4″ to weather.

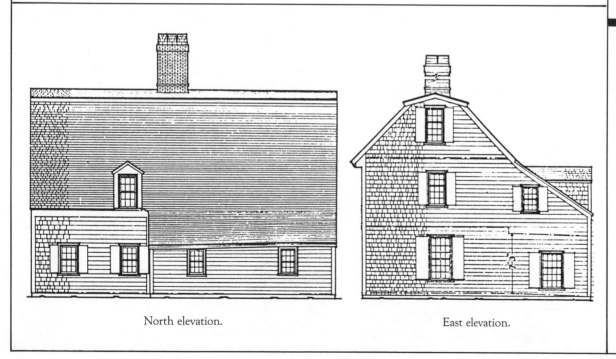

North elevation.

East elevation.

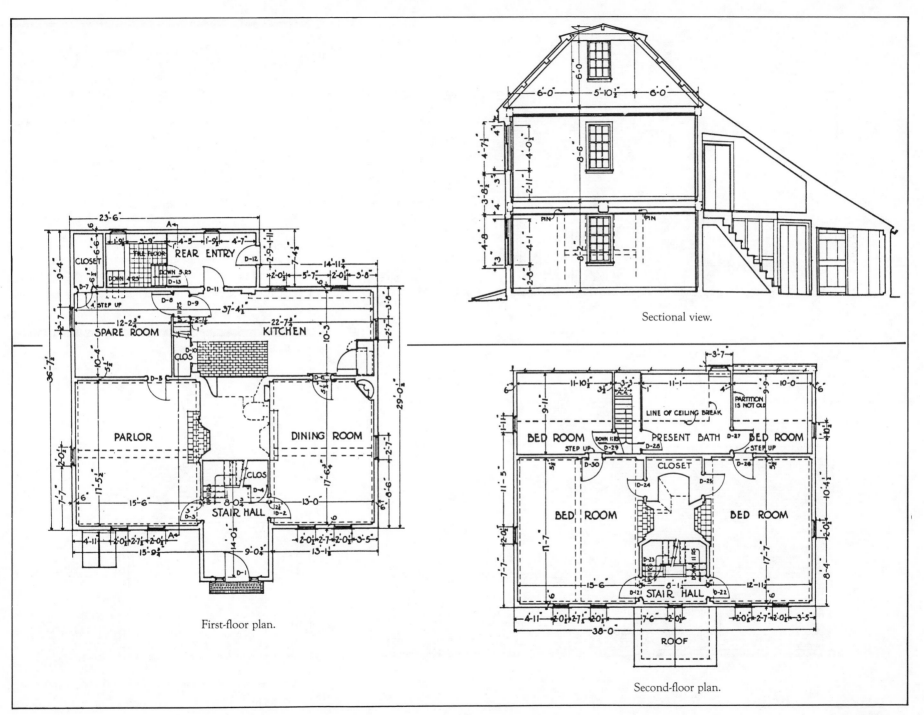

Sectional view.

First-floor plan.

Second-floor plan.

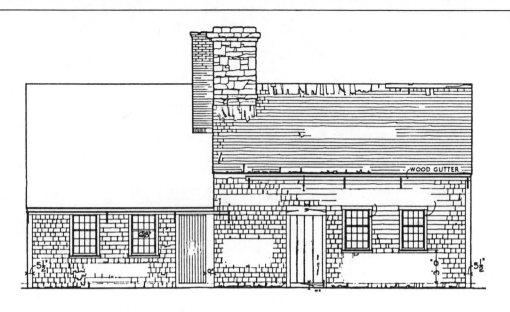

South (front) elevation.

3. **Waite-Potter House**, South Westport, Massachusetts, 1677, 1760. Built in two sections, the larger being the original building, this residence is representative of a type known as a stone-ender in Southeastern Massachusetts and Rhode Island. Most of the original west gable wall is of stone and contains a massive cooking fireplace and oven. When the wing was added, a brick stack was built alongside the stone chimney. The window sash as shown on the front elevation are original. Wood shingling was used in both sections except for the south or front façade; the two roofs were originally wood-shingled.

Just how the interior space was used is not entirely clear, although it would appear that the first building was simply a one-room dwelling with attic space for sleeping. At first, a ladder on the wall was used to reach this level; later, a stairway was cut out in the northeast corner of the room. A second set of stairs winds up alongside the chimney in the addition.

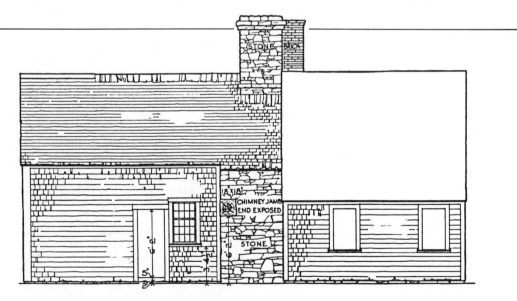

North elevation.

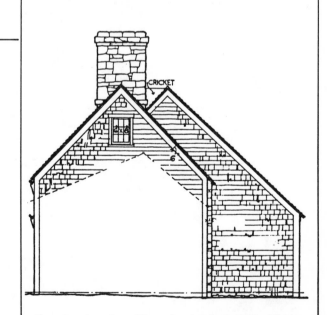

East elevation, dotted lines showing later shed addition.

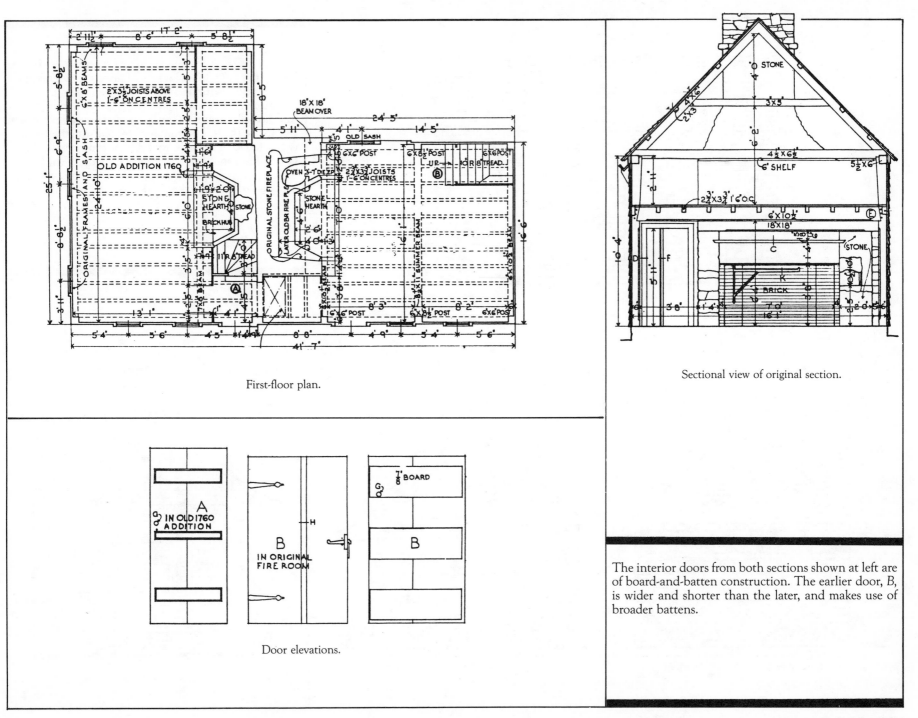

First-floor plan.

Sectional view of original section.

Door elevations.

The interior doors from both sections shown at left are of board-and-batten construction. The earlier door, *B*, is wider and shorter than the later, and makes use of broader battens.

South (front) elevation.

4. **Samuel Desmarest House**, New Milford, New Jersey, c. 1679. Although renovated several times in the 1800s, the Dutch Colonial Desmarest residence has stoutly resisted fundamental change. The coarsed red sandstone walls are difficult to alter, although the rear wall did collapse and was replaced by a frame and shingled wall in the 1890s. The building's most distinctive feature is the flared-eave gable roof which protects the front façade. It overhangs another typical feature of the Dutch Colonial dwelling—a wooden stoop. Thatch, and not shingles, originally covered the roof.

East elevation (before restoration).

West elevation (before restoration).

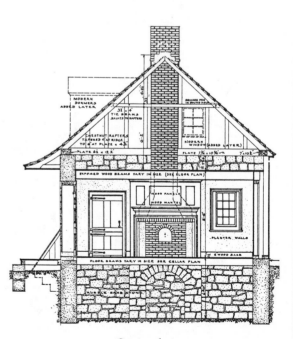

Sectional view.

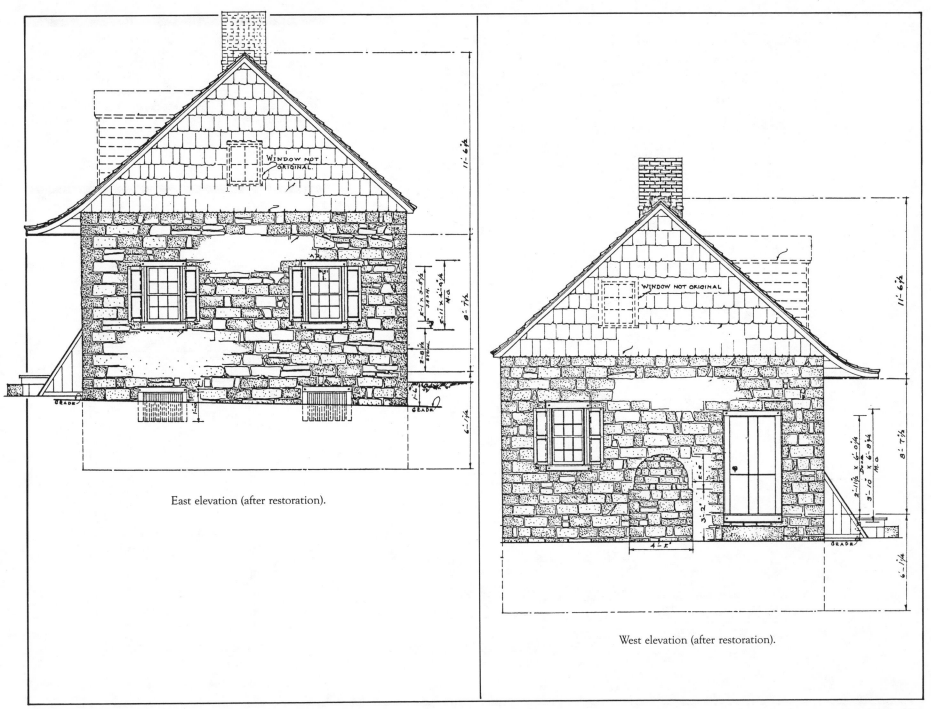

East elevation (after restoration).

West elevation (after restoration).

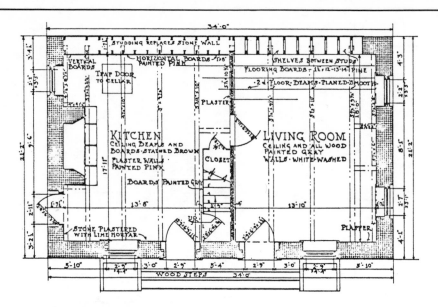

First-floor plan.

As the floor plan shows, the first floor of the Desmarest House was divided into two rooms—a large kitchen and living room. There is evidence in the cellar that two fireplaces—one at each gable end—were planned, but only one chimney stack was built. A large cooking fireplace now stands in the kitchen, and it contains a restored beehive oven.

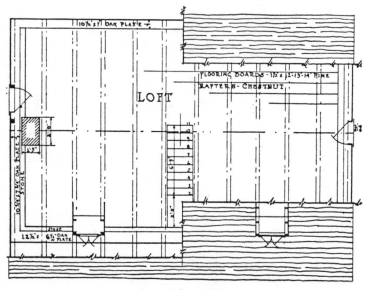

Second-floor plan.

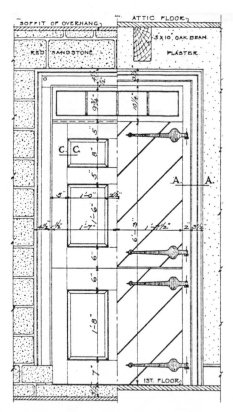

Entrance door (after restoration): *left*, exterior; *right*, interior.

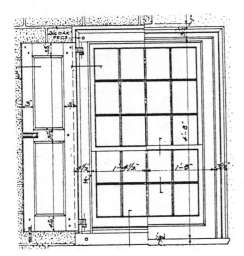

Front window detail: *left*, exterior; *right*, interior.

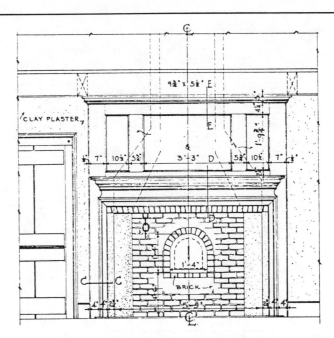

Fireplace elevation (after restoration).

A comparison of the east and west elevations before and after restoration shows the addition of the oven, the replacement of gable pine siding with hand-hewn shingles, a board-and-batten side door with a double Dutch frame door, and the proper resizing of a window. Dormers and gable windows, although not original, were retained as they help to light and enlarge the second-floor space. The two front doors as seen in the elevation on p. 16 date from 1861 and have been replaced with double Dutch doors.

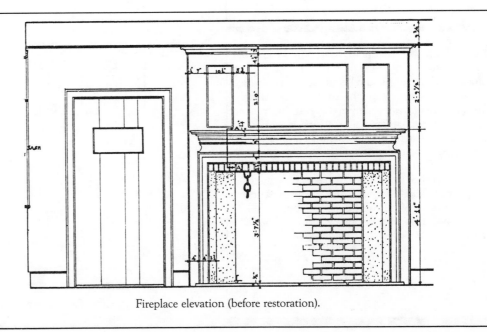

Fireplace elevation (before restoration).

South (front) elevation.

East elevation.

5. **The Peak House**, Medfield, Massachusetts, 1680. An amazing surviving example of early building technology, this building would be difficult to reproduce today because of its very steep gable roof and special framing. Although much restored over the years, according to conjecture and not hard and fast evidence, the building has retained its almost medieval roof line. Later sash windows have been replaced with much smaller casement types, and a paneled entrance door has given way to an earlier portcullis type worthy of a fortress. Considering that the town Medfield was burned to the ground by Indians four years before the house was built, such a fortified entrance may be appropriate if not historically correct.

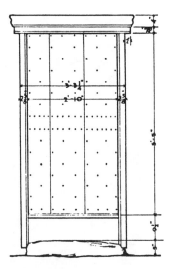

Entrance elevation.

West elevation.

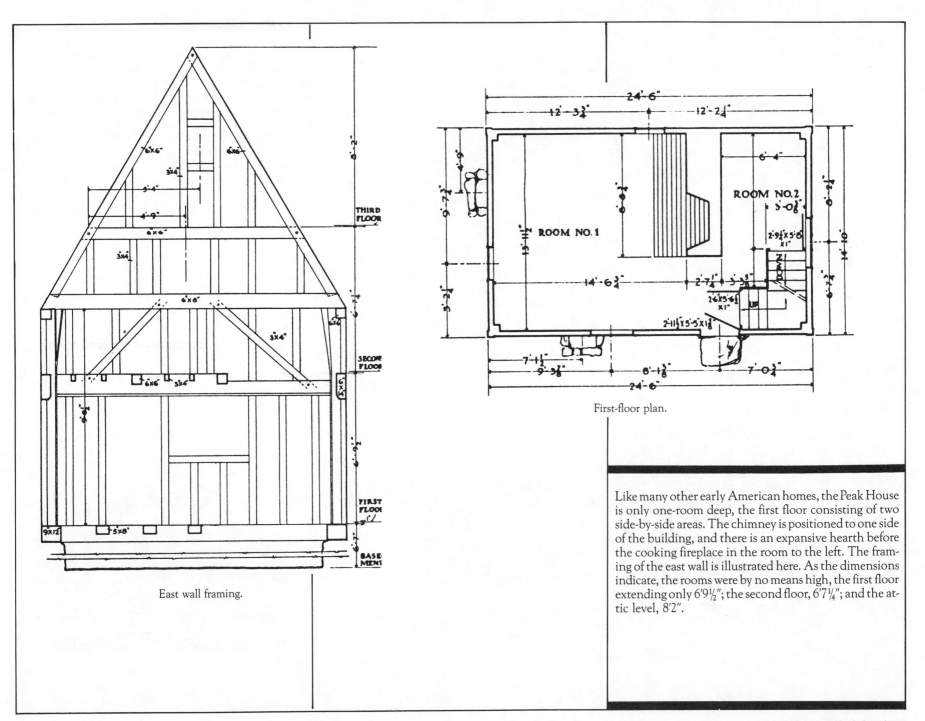

East wall framing.

First-floor plan.

Like many other early American homes, the Peak House is only one-room deep, the first floor consisting of two side-by-side areas. The chimney is positioned to one side of the building, and there is an expansive hearth before the cooking fireplace in the room to the left. The framing of the east wall is illustrated here. As the dimensions indicate, the rooms were by no means high, the first floor extending only 6'9½"; the second floor, 6'7¼"; and the attic level, 8'2".

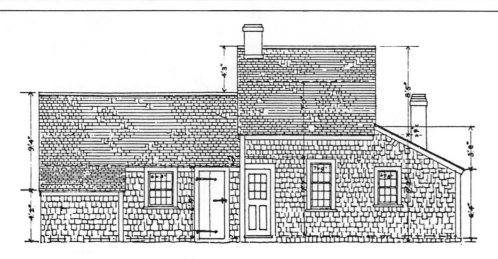

East (front) elevation.

6. **Betsy Cary Cottage**, Siasconset, Massachusetts, 1682, 1782. An appealing fisherman's cottage, this building was built in three sections, the two main sections a century apart. To them was added an even later lean-to. Like many contemporary New England house designs such as those produced by Acorn Structures, the building is an interesting assembly of rectangular units and sheds. The original section, the lower part at left in the front elevation, may itself have been put together in three parts—a shed on each side of a rectangle. The original chimney has disappeared, a new stack having been built in the later living room. A second chimney serves the lean-to kitchen.

West elevation.

North elevation.

There was little sleeping space in the attic of the original section, and how one reached this level is not known; it may have been by ladder. The new section has two good-sized bedrooms reached by a set of stairs built alongside the chimney.

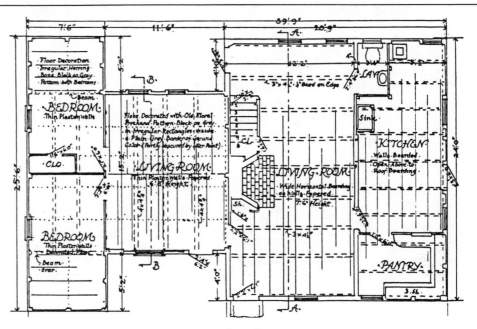

First-floor plan.

South elevation.

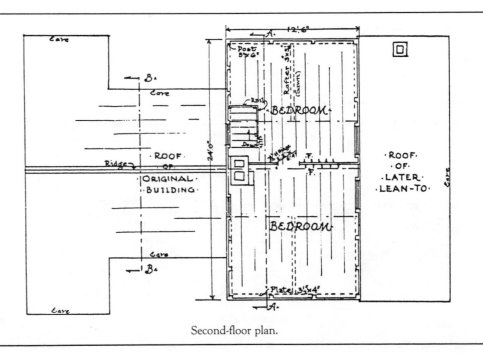

Second-floor plan.

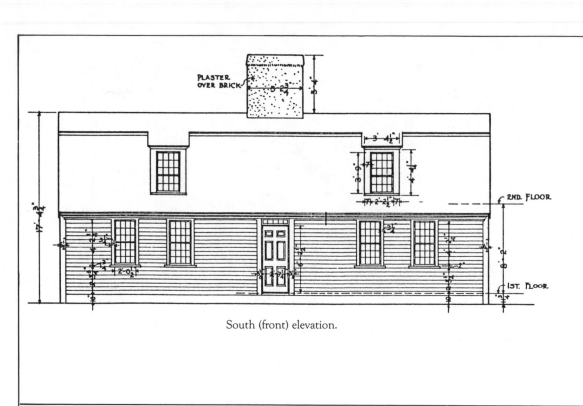

South (front) elevation.

7. **M'am Lee Cottage**, Manchester, Massachusetts, c. 1725. The Lee residence is a classic gambrel-roof New England Colonial building. The original building was of two rooms—a hall and parlor—the shed kitchen having been added later. As is evident from the first-floor plan, each of the original rooms had a large fireplace and oven. Whether the second-story dormers are original is not known. Evidence suggests, however, that the exterior walls were not framed with corner posts, but that the clapboards were laid from corner to corner. The roof and dormers are shingled, as was probably the case originally.

The interior finishing is plain but handsome. Corner cupboards are built in units in the two principal first-floor rooms. On the second floor the ceiling and floor of each bedroom are finished in beaded pine boards running from 15" to 17" in width. Both vertical and horizontal pine paneling also appears on the side walls.

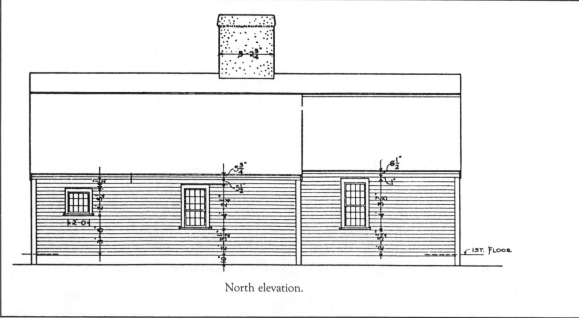

North elevation.

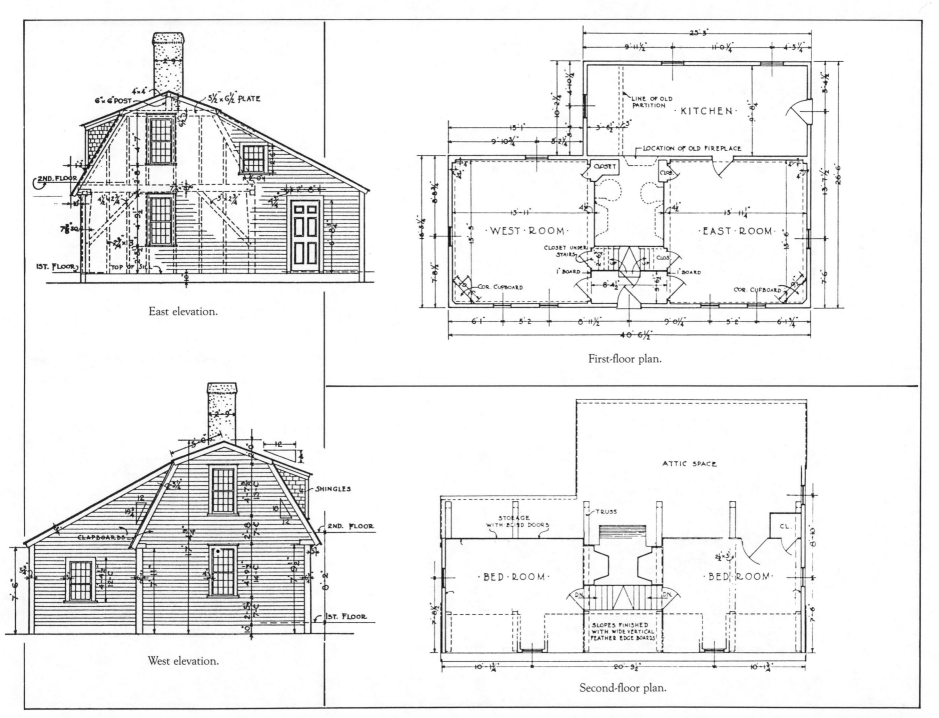

East elevation.

First-floor plan.

West elevation.

Second-floor plan.

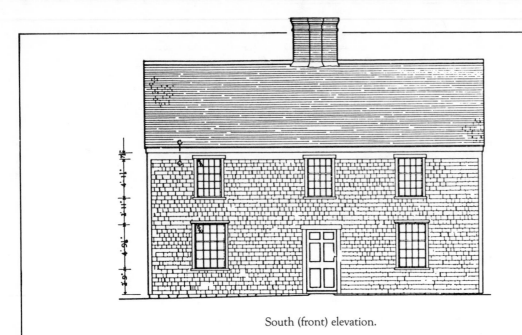

South (front) elevation.

8. **Elihu Coleman House**, Nantucket, Massachusetts, 1722. Another typical center-hall New England Colonial, the Coleman salt-box could very well serve as an admirable model for a modern reproduction. The floor plan has been altered to include a modern bath; the rooms are commodious and the attic floor has enough height to allow for the addition of more bedrooms. The rear kitchen shed, probably a summer kitchen originally, could be used in various ways today—for a utility room, study, or office.

Built at a time when Georgian features were beginning to be used in the colonies, the Coleman House has a relatively sophisticated façade. Corner posts frame the dwelling; a wide cornice wraps around the eaves and the front windows; windows are simply but handsomely framed; and the house is crowned with superb chimney caps.

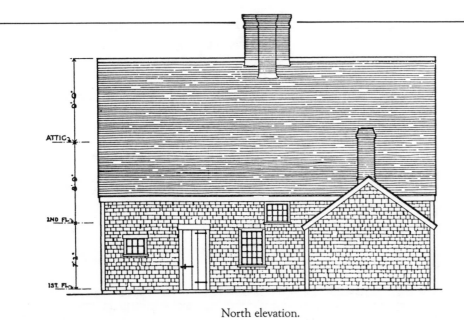

North elevation.

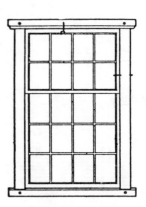

Typical first-floor window elevation.

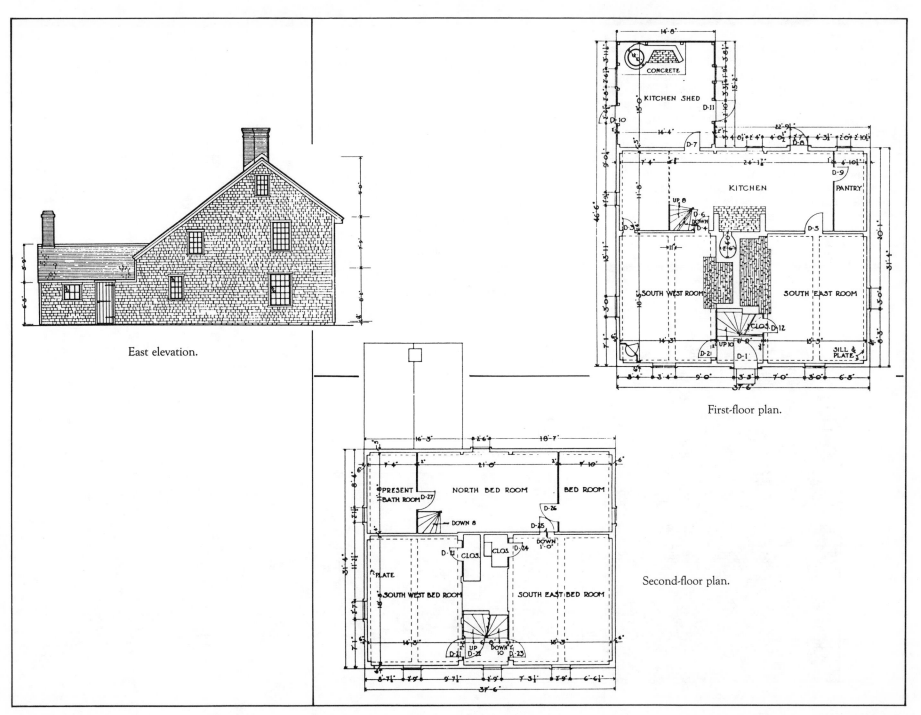

East elevation.

CONCRETE

KITCHEN SHED

D-11

D-10

D-7

D-6

D-9

KITCHEN

PANTRY

UP 8

D-6

DOWN

D-4

D-3

D-5

SOUTH WEST ROOM

SOUTH EAST ROOM

CLOS. D-12

D-21

UP 10

D-1

SILL & PLATE

First-floor plan.

PRESENT BATH ROOM

D-27

NORTH BED ROOM

BED ROOM

DOWN 8

D-26

D-25

DOWN 1'-0"

D-22

CLOS

CLOS

D-24

PLATE

SOUTH WEST BED ROOM

SOUTH EAST BED ROOM

D-21

UP

DOWN 10

D-23

Second-floor plan.

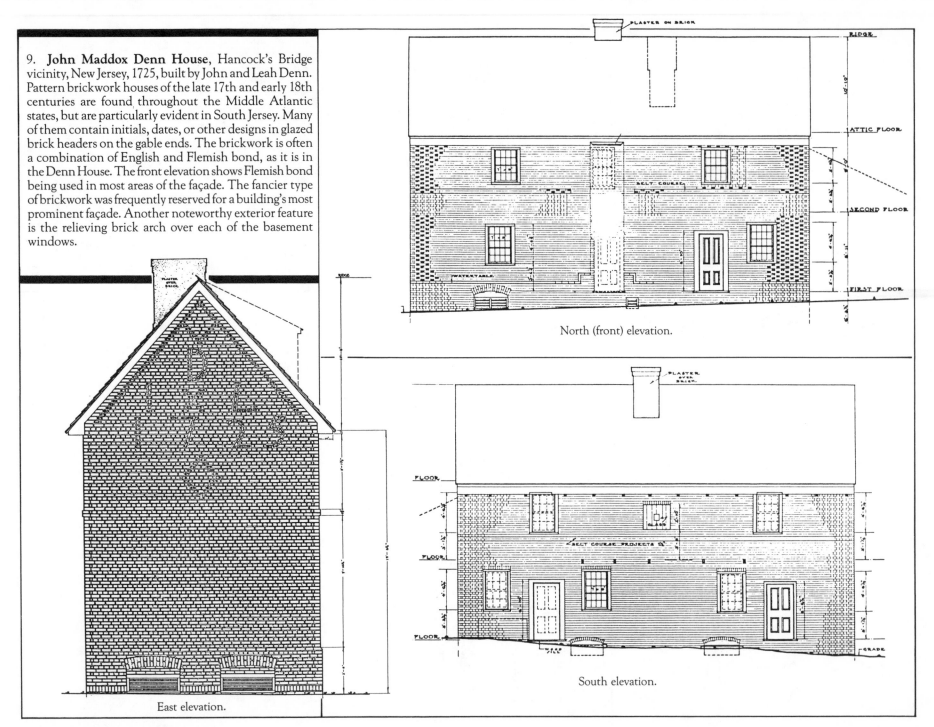

9. **John Maddox Denn House**, Hancock's Bridge vicinity, New Jersey, 1725, built by John and Leah Denn. Pattern brickwork houses of the late 17th and early 18th centuries are found throughout the Middle Atlantic states, but are particularly evident in South Jersey. Many of them contain initials, dates, or other designs in glazed brick headers on the gable ends. The brickwork is often a combination of English and Flemish bond, as it is in the Denn House. The front elevation shows Flemish bond being used in most areas of the façade. The fancier type of brickwork was frequently reserved for a building's most prominent façade. Another noteworthy exterior feature is the relieving brick arch over each of the basement windows.

North (front) elevation.

South elevation.

East elevation.

The original first-floor plan is similar to that found in an early New England house—one-room deep, two rooms wide, and with a front entry hall. The center chimney provides fireplaces for each of the rooms except for one of the second-floor bedrooms, probably a later division of space. The front windows, illustrated here, have 9-over-8 sash and are simply framed.

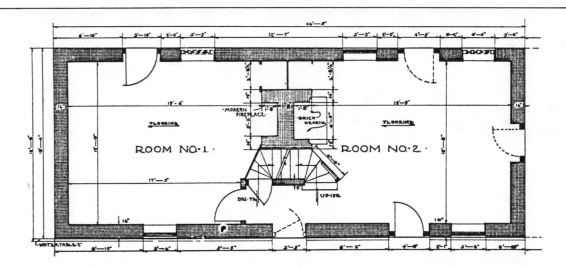

First-floor plan.

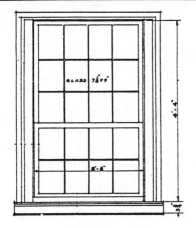

Front first-floor window elevation: *above*, interior; *below*, exterior.

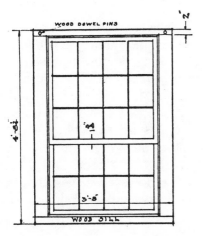

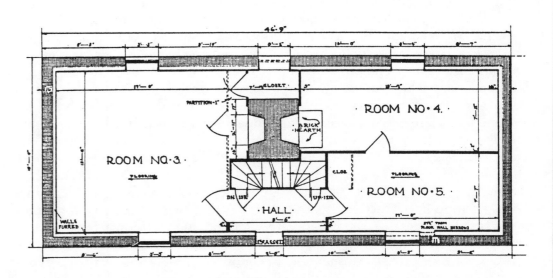

Second-floor plan.

Mid-Colonial

The mid-Colonial house of the early to mid-1700s is principally distinguished from the early Colonial dwelling by Georgian detailing. This is seen most strikingly in the main entrance, which is often handsomely defined by such details as a pediment, pilasters, columns, fluted moldings, or a combination thereof. The entry door itself is made up of molded panels rather than battens and boards. Other differences are larger windows, use of quoins or corner posts and a cornice, a precise symmetrical arrangement of doors and windows, and, in the interior, use of various moldings and other decorative trim.

The mid-Colonial house is usually a larger building than the earlier Colonial and is often two-rooms rather than one-room deep and two or two-and-a-half rather than one-and-a-half stories high. Dormers and small windows at the gable ends light the attic space. Sliding sash of multiple lights takes the place of casement windows with diamond panes.

The Daniel Gould House (pp. 44-45) is a model Georgian Colonial frame residence of the mid-18th century. The chimney is still centered, and this position largely determines the room layout. The salt-box, however, is much wider than the average early Colonial, and provision was made for a separate kitchen and pantry. New England buildings of this type have served as the inspiration for countless reproductions today. It is large enough to serve a small family and can be adapted easily to include modern needs.

Many buildings built during the first half of the 18th century are not as strikingly Georgian in appearance. What they have in common is a decorative main entrance and a balanced distribution of windows and doors. The Ackerman House (pp. 36-37) and the Jacobus House (pp. 52-53) are both northeast New Jersey Dutch Colonial buildings with distinctive flaring eaves. Both houses are distinguished from the first period of Colonial building by the decorative treatment of doors and windows. The Ackerman House is also laid out around a central hall, a feature not found in many English Colonial houses until the mid- to late 18th century when two chimneys near each gable end replaced the use of a center chimney.

The Miller's House (pp. 50-51) in western New Jersey is thoroughly Georgian in composition, but in size and floor plan is reminiscent of the early English hall/parlor plan dwelling. Because it is built on a hillside, however, more use is made of the basement level. Such stone dwellings are often called German bank houses. Whether they were indeed built by German immigrant masons or by others of a different background who adopted the German model is hard to determine. That such buildings existed in German-speaking areas of Europe during the time of emigration is certain. The framing of the doors and windows and their very symmetrical arrangement, however, suggest that this house and many others like it were the product of builders well versed in various building traditions.

10. **Venus Thompson House**, Middleboro, Massachusetts, c. 1700. A handsomely framed dwelling, this house carries some distinctive early Georgian details. The entrance with pilasters and sidelights is beautifully scaled; corner posts, baseboards, and a cornice neatly define the structure.

Shingles rather than clapboard siding originally covered the walls; the roof is, and was, shingled. The windows are not original, but how they differ is not known.

The room layout is quite unusual for such a foursquare house. The area now designated the living room was the original kitchen. A substantial chimney allows for a cooking fireplace and oven on the kitchen side and another fireplace on the sitting room side. A second chimney at the other side of the house provides a fireplace for the parlor.

There is only one bedroom on the second floor, but at least another bedroom could be created out of the remaining central floor space. At one time this area must have been used more fully, as the fireplace located here was originally open.

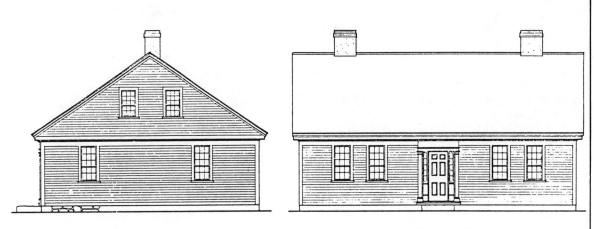

North elevation.

East (front) elevation.

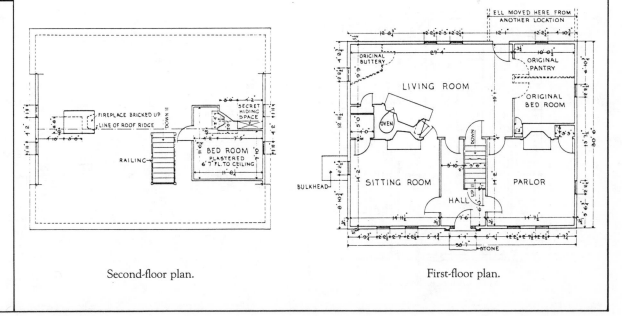

Second-floor plan.

First-floor plan.

11. Francis Wyman House, Burlington, Massachusetts, 1666. How this building appeared soon after it was built is not known, but it certainly modified in the early 1700s. The regular wood blocks serving as quoins on all four sides are probably original to the house. Both the main and side entrances with fluted pilasters appear to have been alterations. The central chimney is of massive construction and at one time provided flues for as many as six fireplaces; two of these have been cemented over. Front and back sets of stairs run alongside the chimney, the back set connecting only the second and attic floors.

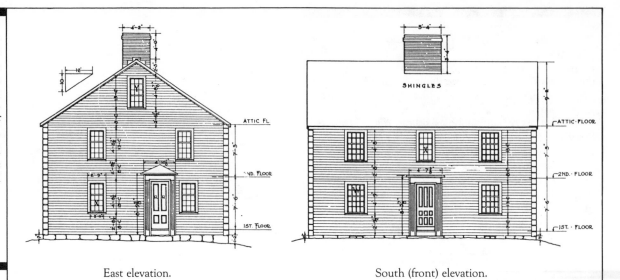

East elevation.

South (front) elevation.

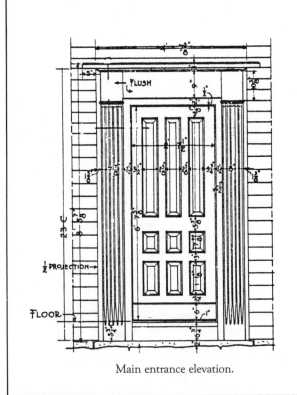

Main entrance elevation.

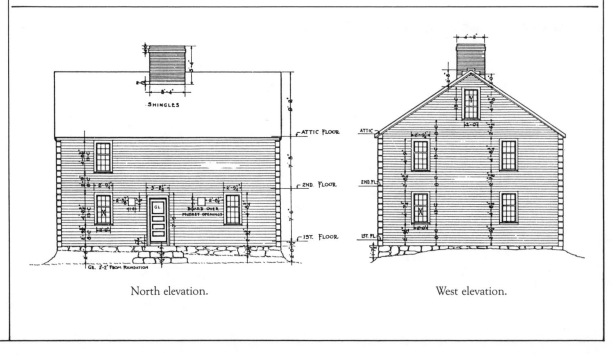

North elevation.

West elevation.

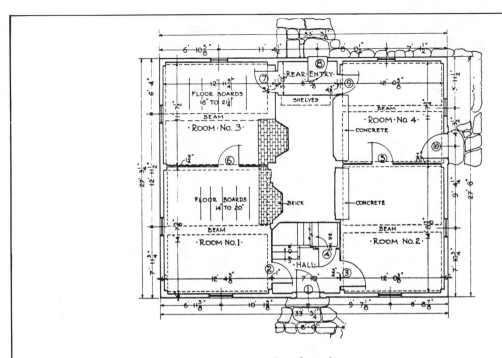

First-floor plan.

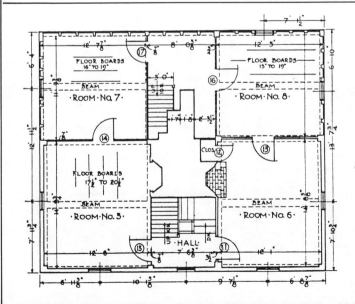

Second-floor plan.

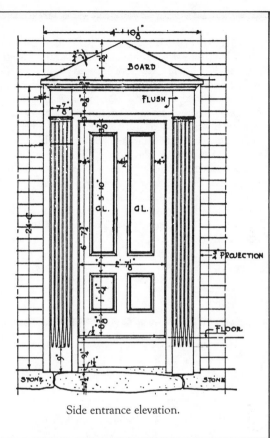

Side entrance elevation.

Main entrance sectional view.

12. **Bryant Cushing House**, Norwell, Massachusetts, 1698. Distinguished by a pedimented and pilastered entrance, the Cushing residence would please a gentleman of any generation. The elegant entrance is properly proportioned for the 40'9" x 30'8" symmetrical rectangle that forms the earliest and main section of the house; side and rear sheds were added later. Other architectural elements of special note are the handsomely framed 12-over-12 windows of the front façade and the three-flue, capped brick center chimney. At one time the windows were probably shuttered. The walls and roof are shingled.

A leaded glass window at the rear of the house, seen below, is said not to be original to the building. The glass in both this window and the bull's-eye panes of the entrance transom is English, but of the same period as the house.

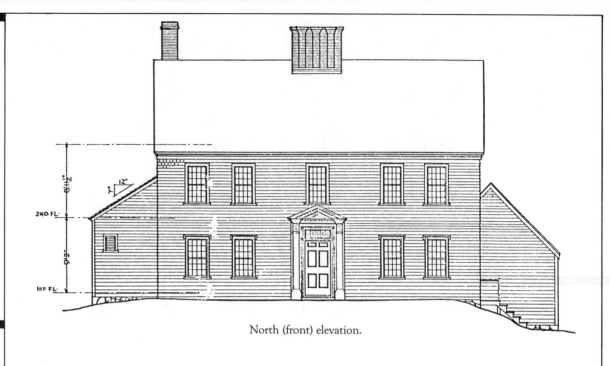

North (front) elevation.

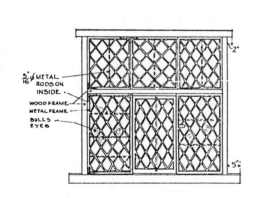

Elevation of leaded glass window.

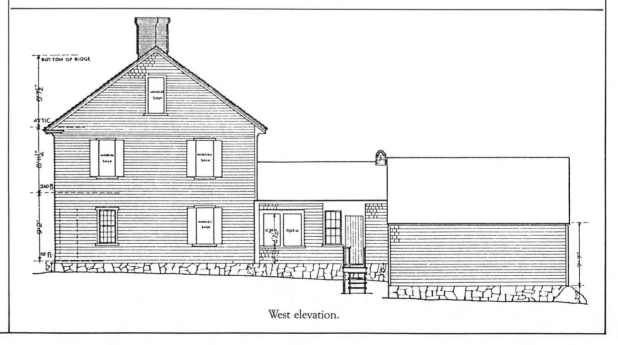

West elevation.

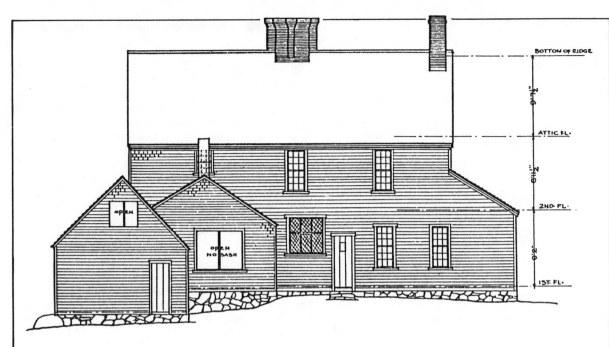

South elevation.

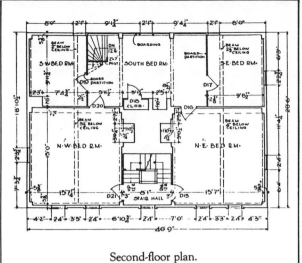

Second-floor plan.

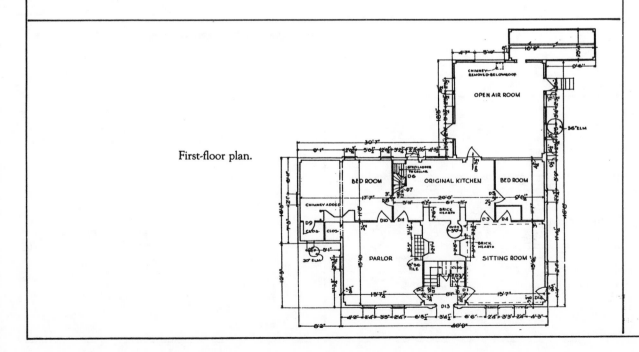

First-floor plan.

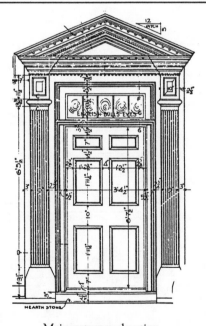

Main entrance elevation.

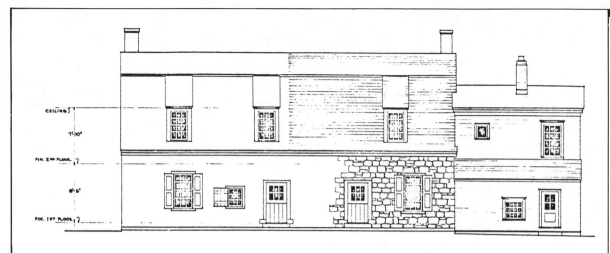

North elevation.

13. Ackerman (Brinckerhoff) House, Hackensack, New Jersey, c. 1696-1704. A typical Dutch Colonial of the New Jersey/New York area, this house grew in three and perhaps four stages. These are discernable in the first-floor plan and elevations: the stone area to the right in the north elevation could have been built in two sections; the shingled frame service wing at left, except for a c. 1865 shed (laundry), was an early 19th-century addition. It is curious to find that a bearing wall of the same thickness as the present exterior stone walls divides the dining room and alcove from the hall. Yet, as is evident from the elevation drawings, the stonework is knit together in a uniform manner. And the gambrel gable with flaring eaves, a distinctive feature of many Dutch Colonial dwellings, forms a continuous line across the entire stone portion.

The room layout overall is very generous. In the main section, all rooms may be entered from a 10'-wide hall, a space open from the front of the house to the rear. The service wing has its own set of stairs off the kitchen. On the wing's second floor are two small bedrooms that suggest servants were in residence by the early 1800s.

South (front) elevation.

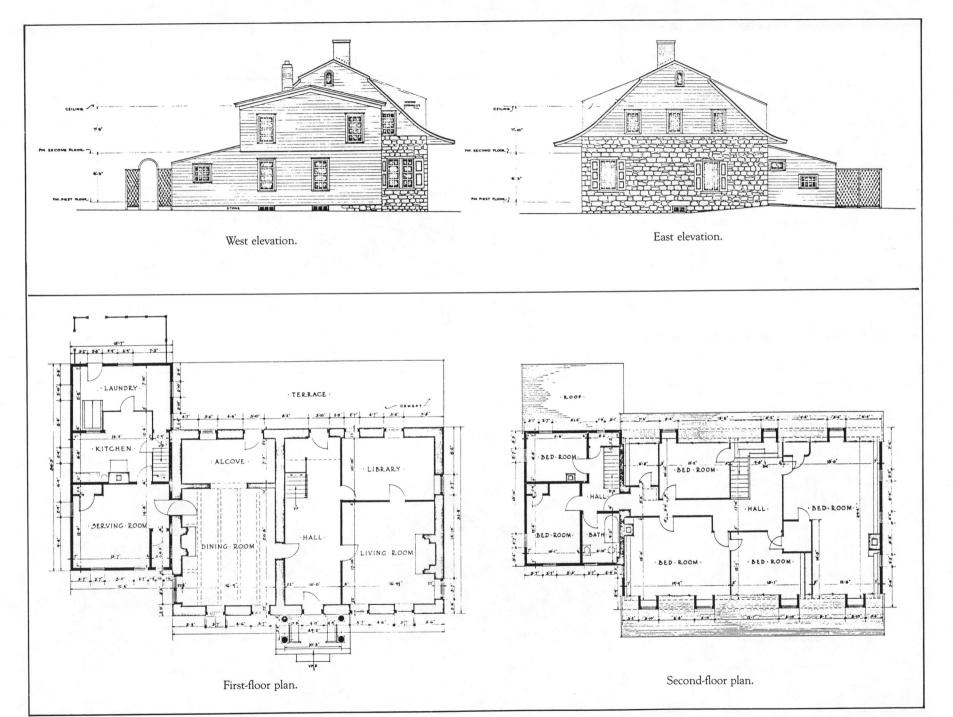

West elevation.

East elevation.

First-floor plan.

Second-floor plan.

LAUNDRY

KITCHEN

SERVING·ROOM

ALCOVE

DINING·ROOM

TERRACE

HALL

LIBRARY

LIVING·ROOM

ROOF

BED·ROOM

HALL

BED·ROOM

BATH

BED·ROOM

BED·ROOM

HALL

BED·ROOM

BED·ROOM

14. **Shadrach Standish House**, Halifax, Massachusetts, c. 1730. The design of this small center-chimney Colonial is very pleasing. A pilastered front entrance is a gracious feature; windows, corners, and eaves are simply but handsomely framed. Both 6-over-6 and 12-over-12 sash are used; presumably, those with a greater number of panes are older. The kitchen is now found in a rear addition (not shown), having formerly occupied the space now designated as the living room. Since there are already two spacious parlors in the front of the house, it would seem suitable to use the living room as a dining room, if so desired. The original pantry is still located to one side.

The two first-floor bedrooms are very small; one could be used as a utility room or modern bath. Full use is not made of the second floor. Even though the ceiling height is only 6'10", this is more than sufficient height for most modern family members.

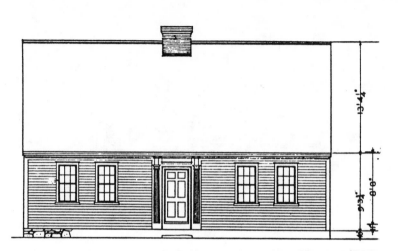

East (front) elevation.

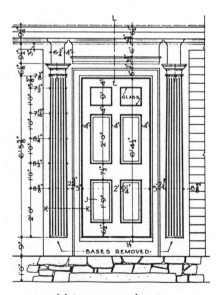

Main entrance elevation.

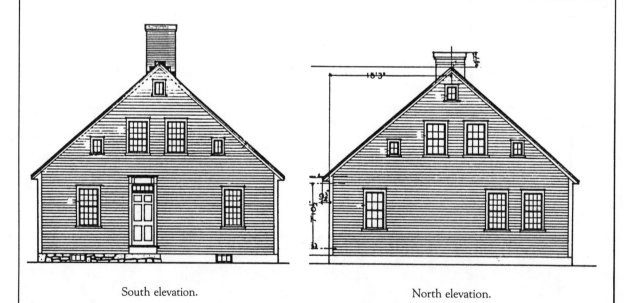

South elevation.

North elevation.

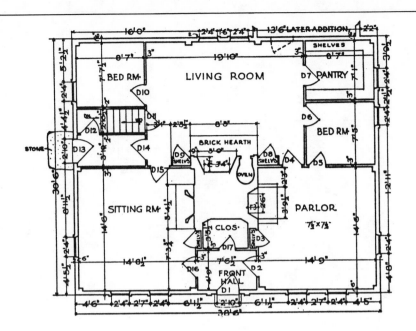

First-floor plan.

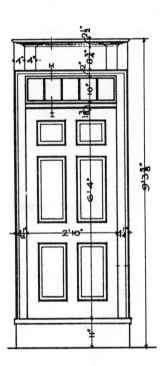

South (side) entrance elevation.

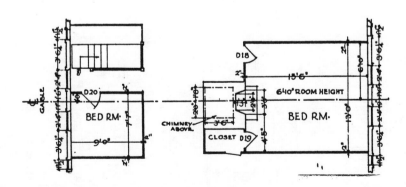

Second-floor plan.

15. **Barnaby House**, Freetown, Massachusetts, c. 1740. The Barnaby dwelling was built in two stages, and, most unusually for an old house, was reduced in size at a later time. The first section probably comprised what is now designated on the first-floor plan as the south parlor, stair hall, kitchen, and pantry. An old window frame is covered up in what was the north exterior wall of this original section. The floor space was approximately tripled and the house was transformed into a Georgian Colonial in the second stage. Fourteen feet of this addition were removed in about 1914.

This reduction in size resulted in the interior being strangely chopped up. The area around the north rear chimney, for example, was left without any real practical use. In most of the rooms, fireplaces and hearths were removed. These, however, can always be restored.

West elevation.

East (front) elevation.

North elevation.

First-floor plan.

South elevation.

Second-floor plan.

16. **Daniel Gould House**, Boxford, Massachusetts, 1740. With a pillared and pedimented porch entrance, the Gould residence was stylish for its time. Because of the building's fine regular lines and framing of all elements, it is a model Georgian Colonial worthy of imitation today. The basic form is that of a salt-box with a later rear side extension. Dormers were also added to the rear at a later date.

The center chimney is of massive construction. At one time it served the sitting room, parlor, and kitchen, as well as the two second-floor bedrooms. A buttery, located next to the kitchen, served in the Colonial period as a pantry for the storage of kitchen equipment as well as a place to keep dairy products. In the average Colonial kitchen, utensils were only hung overhead if there was no other place to store them.

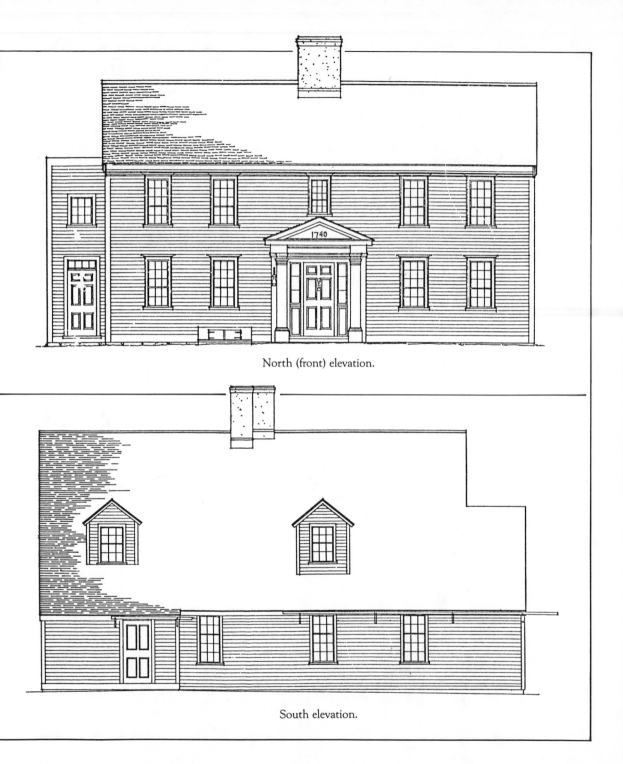

North (front) elevation.

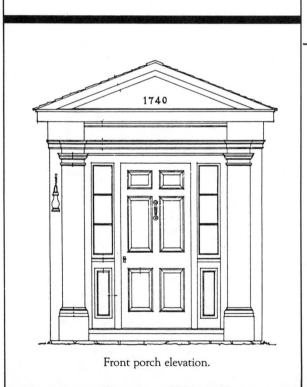

Front porch elevation.

South elevation.

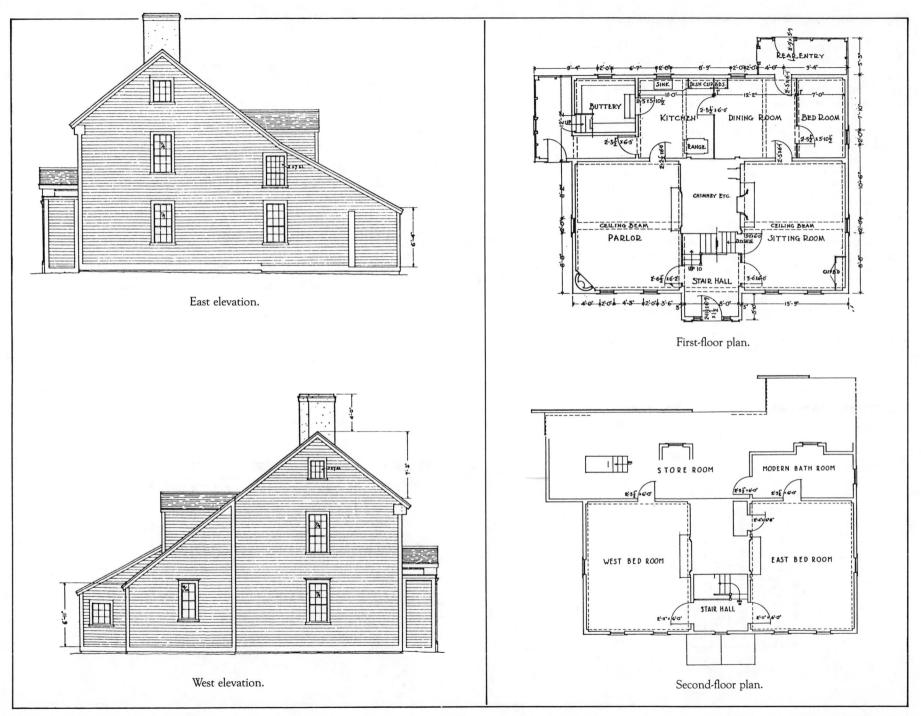

East elevation.

West elevation.

First-floor plan.

Second-floor plan.

17. **The Old Red House**, Gill, Massachusetts, c. 1745. Given its name because of red-painted clapboards and trim, this compact mid-Colonial house is, from exterior appearances, a perfectly traditional building. The windows and main entrance are neatly tucked into the cornice. All the architectural elements are symmetrically arranged in the original rectangular building as well as in the later wing. Inside, however, one discovers that the house really has two main entrances. There is no stairway in what was the original south front section and only a shallow front hall containing a long closet along the chimney wall. The main stairway is arranged to the rear of the house at one side of a wide hall. The side or second main entrance leads into this hall. When the wing was added, it would appear that the orientation of the house was changed as well. Was there ever a front stairway? Probably, but evidence is lacking now.

As is common in many other Colonial houses with steeply-pitched roofs, the second-floor bedrooms occupy only part of the second-floor space. The areas closest to the eaves are kept for open storage, and the center is occupied by the chimney and a hall.

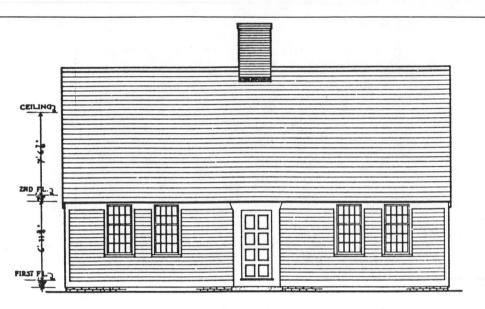

South (front) elevation.

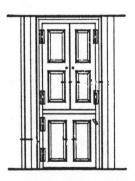

Dining room corner cupboard elevation.

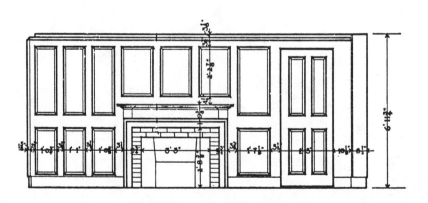

Paneled dining room end elevation.

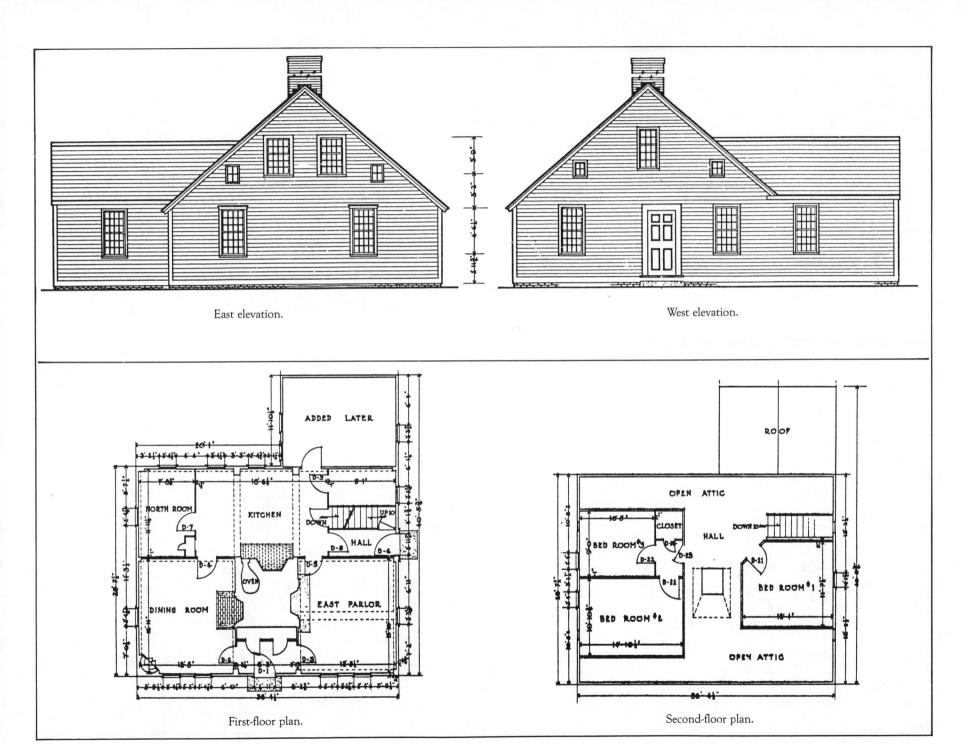

East elevation.

West elevation.

First-floor plan.

Second-floor plan.

18. **The Lutkins House**, Rochelle Park, New Jersey, 1760. This very modest dwelling might be better termed a cottage than a house. Yet, within it, most needs of an 18th-century couple or small family were met. Today the layout could be adapted to include a modern bath and better access to the second-floor space above the main section. How one reached the second floor is not indicated; a wall ladder may have been the only means. New stairs could be brought up from the hall or parlor.

The exterior features are a mixture of the primitive and the sophisticated. The shutters, for example, are either simple board and batten or the fancier paneled. The main entrance door is a one-piece formal paneled slab, whereas the double Dutch kitchen door is board and batten.

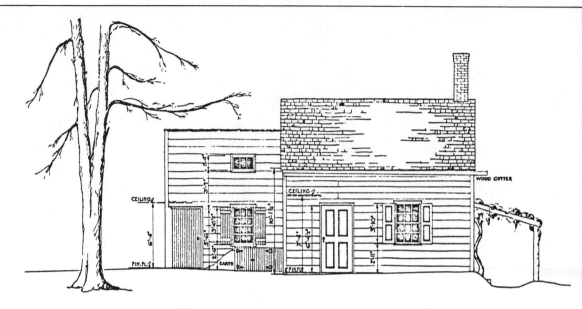

West (front) elevation.

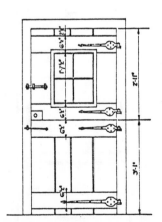

Kitchen door elevation, interior.

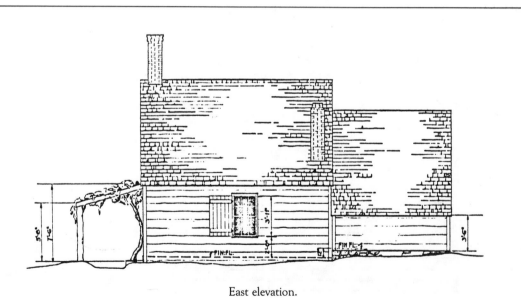

East elevation.

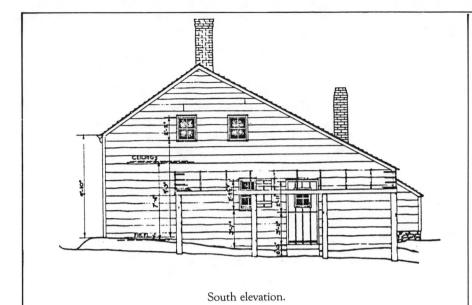

South elevation.

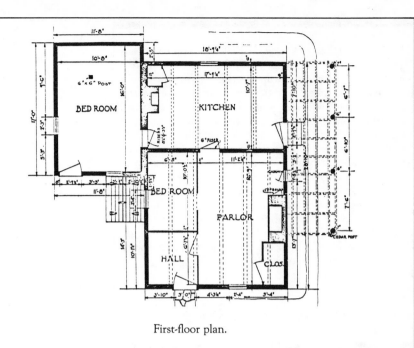

First-floor plan.

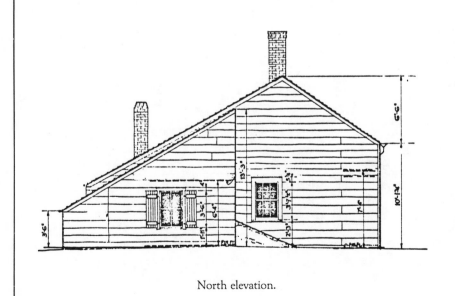

North elevation.

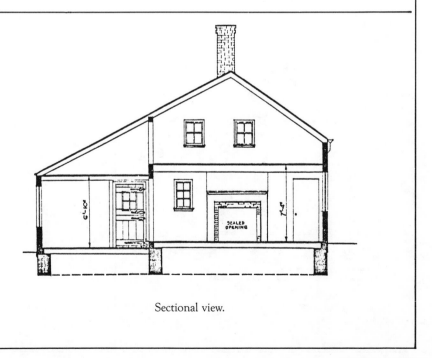

Sectional view.

19. **The Miller's House**, John Opdyke Farm, Sergeantsville, New Jersey, c. 1740. Built in two sections within a relatively short time, this farmhouse probably began life as a three-bay structure. In form, the one-room deep, two-room wide dwelling with chimneys at each end resembles the I-houses of a later period. This type of stone house with 16″-thick walls and deep window and door reveals is typical of houses in the Delaware Valley of New Jersey and Pennsylvania. The building type is particularly prevalent in areas of Quaker settlement. The gable ends have windows only at the attic level; those at the basement level are later additions.

Many of the early farmhouses of this region were built into the side of the hill, as were also barns, and are therefore known as bank houses. The stone walls were usually stuccoed, an early form of insulation.

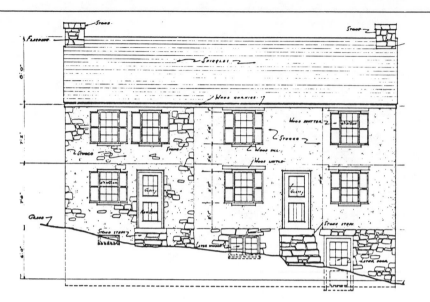

South (front) elevation.

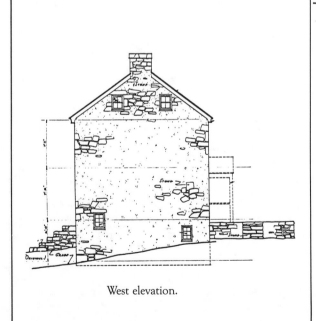

West elevation.

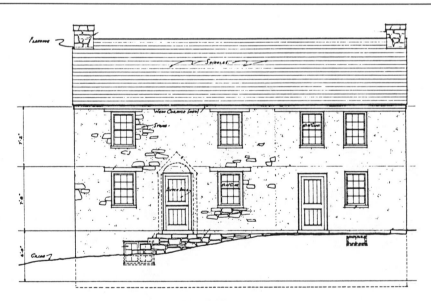

North elevation.

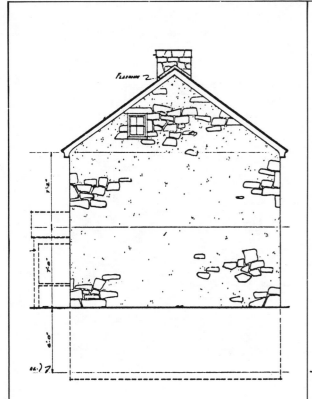

East elevation.

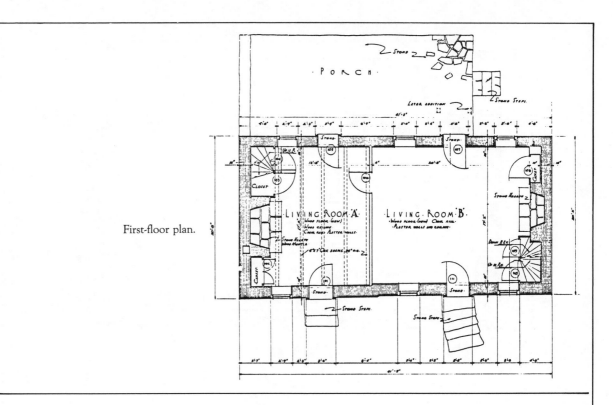

First-floor plan.

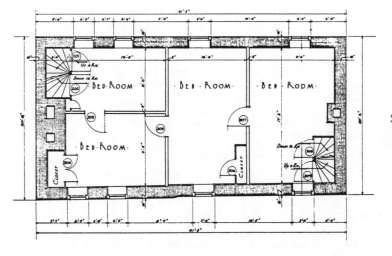

Second-floor plan.

The floor plans indicate the placements of stairways or tight-winders at each gable end. The first-floor room ends are wood paneled (as seen on the following pages) and at one end of the floor a simple shelf over the fireplace serves in place of a mantel.

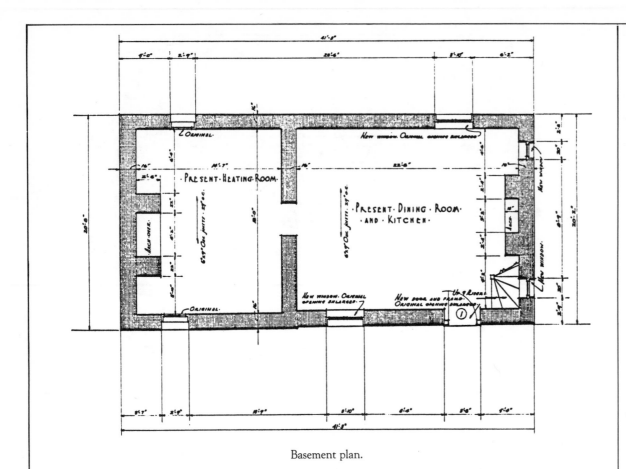

Basement plan.

Sectional view.

West room end elevation.

The basement level, partially above ground level at the back of the house, was often the location of the kitchen, and is so used today. Other space is occupied by heating equipment.

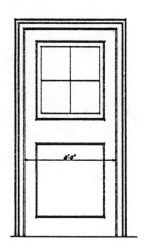

South first-floor door elevation, exterior.

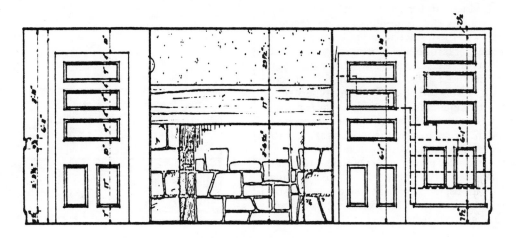

East room end elevation.

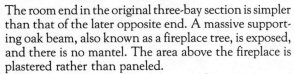

The room end in the original three-bay section is simpler than that of the later opposite end. A massive supporting oak beam, also known as a fireplace tree, is exposed, and there is no mantel. The area above the fireplace is plastered rather than paneled.

The windows on the first and second floors are 6-over-6 sash. An interior feature found in some Delaware Valley stone homes of the period is the placement of a drawer in a window's casing. It is framed by the sill and chair rail.

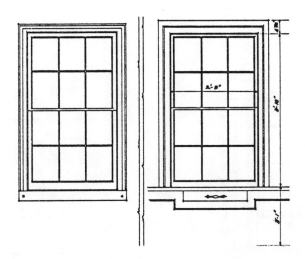

First-floor window elevations: *left*, exterior; *right*, interior.

20. John I. Jacobus House, Towaco, New Jersey, c. 1760. Of fieldstone and frame, this northeast New Jersey dwelling resembles the stone houses of the Delaware Valley farther to the west. The flaring eave of the roof line, however, marks the house as being essentially Dutch Colonial in style. Fieldstone is used for the basement and three of the first-floor walls, the front being of frame construction with clapboard siding. The same type of siding covers the attic gable ends and extends several feet below. Alterations have changed the appearance of this house greatly, and the drawings show the windows as they probably appeared originally. Missing from the building is some sort of stoop or porch and set of stairs to serve the double parlor entrances on the first floor. As seen from the end elevations, the basement wall extends beyond the first-floor level, and there is a protruding beam at each end to serve as a porch support.

South (front) elevation.

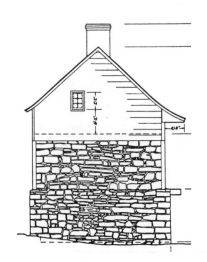

West elevation.

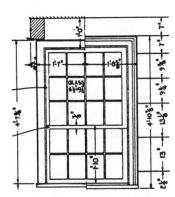

South window elevation, first floor: *left*, interior; *right*, exterior.

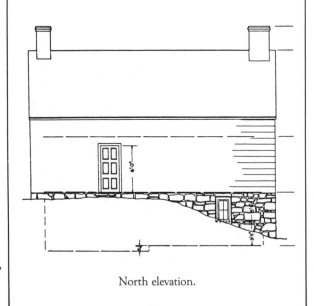

North elevation.

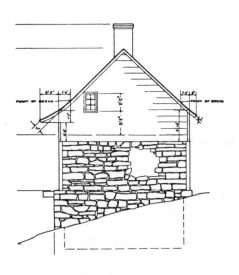

East elevation.

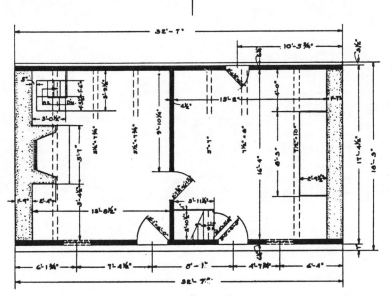

First-floor plan.

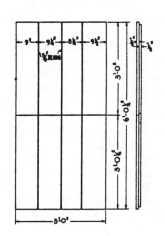

Interior door elevation, first floor.

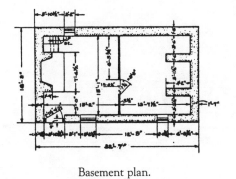

Basement plan.

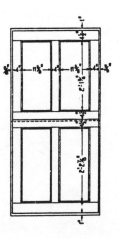

Second-floor plan.

Exterior door elevation, first floor.

21. **Schuyler-Colfax House**, Pompton Lakes vicinity, New Jersey, c. 1712, c. 1735. The dormers and front porch radically change the appearance of the original large section of this house; these are mid-19th century alterations. A better sense of the building's basic Dutch Colonial profile can be gained from studying the side and rear elevations. The gambrel roof then comes into full view. The one-and-a-half story wing was added in 1735 and provided space for a new dining room, kitchen, and a storeroom (also designated as a slave room).

The combination of various building materials—fieldstone, brown sandstone for quoins, brick laid in Flemish bond, and clapboard siding—is unusual, but not without visual appeal. Each of the exterior entrance doors is different, reflecting the various alterations made in the building's nearly 275-year history. The sash in the windows of the rear main section are probably original; elsewhere, of more recent vintage.

The interior is very formal and reflects the taste and interests of a prosperous country gentleman's family. Each of the rooms is well proportioned and contains a fireplace.

East (front) elevation.

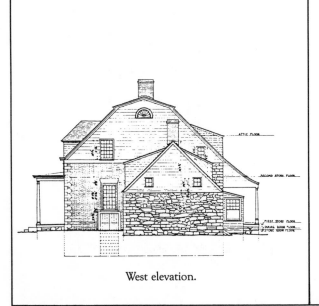

West elevation.

North elevation.

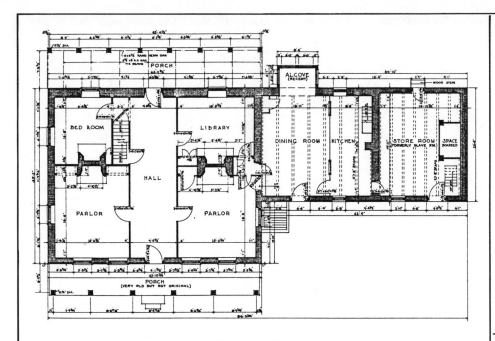

First-floor plan.

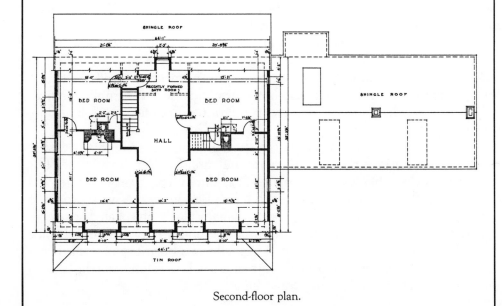

Second-floor plan.

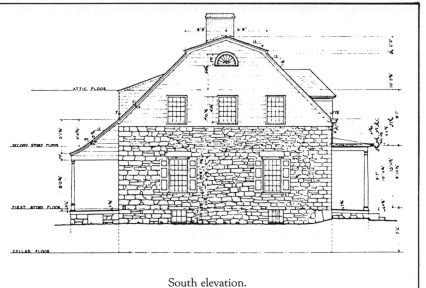

South elevation.

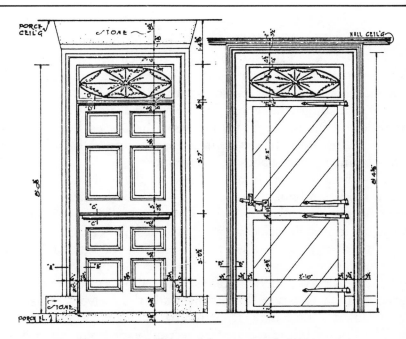

Main entrance elevation: *left,* exterior; *right,* interior.

Late Colonial

The Georgian style in architecture flourished most fully in the second half of the 1700s and persisted in popularity well into the first two decades of the 19th century. Entrances are elaborate and include such elements as sidelights, fanlights or transoms with tracery, and extended porticoes. In some buildings, the center section projects slightly to form a pavilion. Windows are dressed with pediments in the fanciest houses and a dentil cornice of wood blocks defines the roof line. A Palladian window may be incorporated above the entrance.

Two, three, or four chimneys rise from the roof and are positioned on the sides and not at the center. This allows for either a center-hall or side-hall floor plan. In either case, some allowance is made for a spacious front stair hall, if not a floor-through passage. Closet stairs have almost entirely disappeared, their use being consigned principally to a secondary status at the back of the house. Doorways may be framed with bolection or fluted moldings. The ceiling is often set off from the walls with a crown molding, the walls themselves consisting of a paneled area and a dado separated by a chair rail.

The houses illustrated in this section vary from the very simple Woolman House (pp. 55-57), which retains the use of closet stairs, to the fashionable Lighthipe House (pp. 70-72), which has a handsome open main stairway. None of the houses are like the great Georgian mansions built in Philadelphia and Boston or the plantation homes of Maryland and Virginia. They are instead vernacular interpretations of classic designs and not textbook copies. No architect is known for any of these buildings. A carpenter-builder or the owner himself could have turned to a manual for assistance, consulted one of the English sources of classic design for decorative inspiration, or studied a similar house nearby.

Each of the houses presented on the following pages reflects to a greater or lesser degree the prevailing architectural fashion of the time. The Schenck-Polhemus House (pp. 64-65), built by a prosperous farmer, has a first floor which includes both a living room and a sitting room, a genteel arrangement of space. Both rooms display sophisticated ornamentation on the walls and surrounding doors and windows. The Lighthipe House (pp. 70-72), the home of a small-town businessman, illustrates in its interior and exterior appointments just how elaborately the basically late Colonial dwelling could be adorned.

22. John Woolman House, Mount Holly, New Jersey, 1771, with later frame addition. The home the well-known Quaker abolitionist and missionary built for his daughter is now a religious retreat. The exterior, except for a kitchen addition and a new front porch, has changed little over the years. Red brick, laid in Flemish bond, lends the building a stylishness worthy of a fine town house. The building has a simple elegance. It is as if Woolman took to heart the Philadelphia Quaker dictum, "of the best sort, but plain."

The room layout on each of the three floors is straightforward, with every square foot well utilized. The corner fireplaces are an unusual feature. Rather than a center staircase, tightwinders communicate between the basement and the third floor.

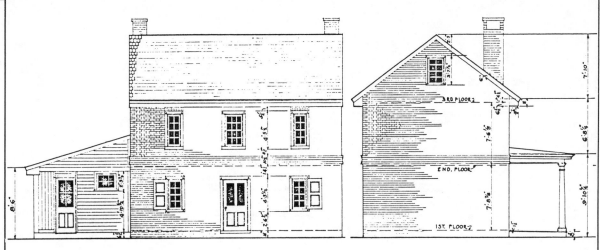

North elevation.

West elevation.

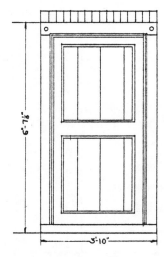

South door elevation, exterior.

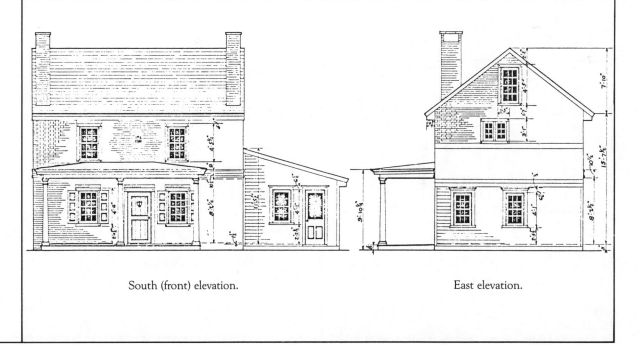

South (front) elevation.

East elevation.

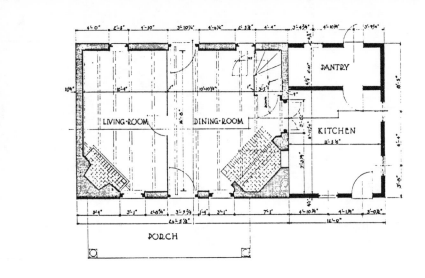

First-floor plan.

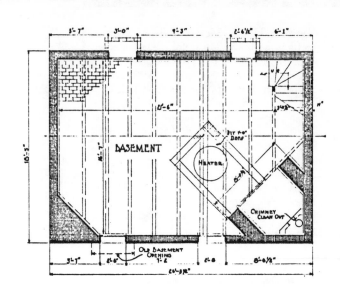

Basement plan.

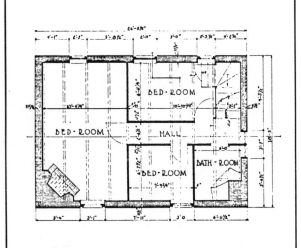

Second-floor plan.

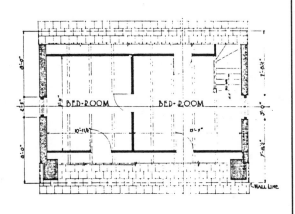

Third-floor plan.

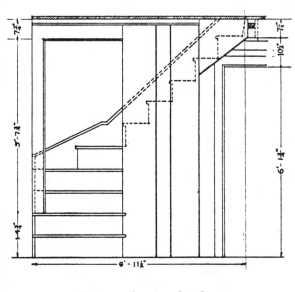

Staircase elevation, first floor.

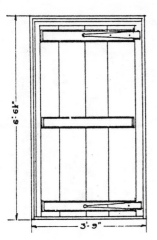

South door elevation, interior.

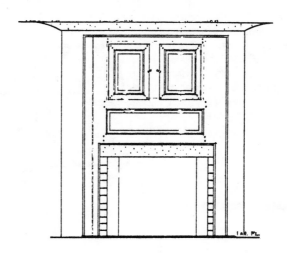

Fireplace wall elevation, living room.

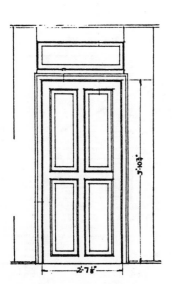

Interior door elevation between living and dining rooms.

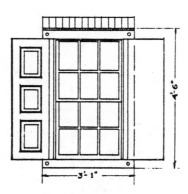

South window elevation, exterior.

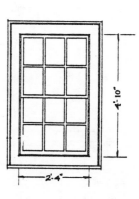

South window elevation, interior.

23. **Michael Kearny Cottage**, Perth Amboy, New Jersey, c. 1784; moved, 1935; remodeled, 1939. Because this building was moved and remodeled, it is difficult to tell what might have been its original form and orientation. The use of brick on the west façade and the placement of the entry hall and center stairway in this section suggest that what is now the rear was once the front of the building. The present dormers are probably later additions, as is the front porch on the east side.

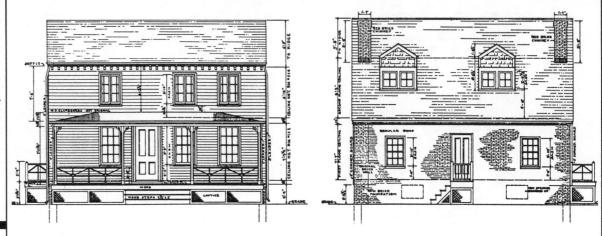

East (front) elevation.

West elevation.

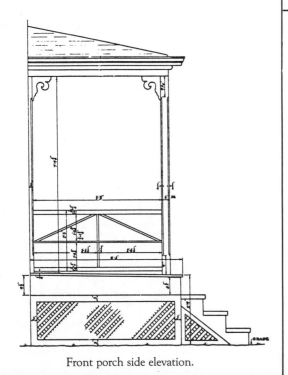

Front porch side elevation.

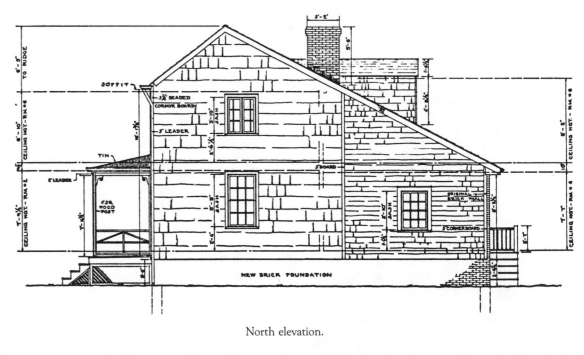

North elevation.

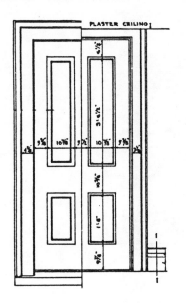

Front entrance elevation:
left, exterior; *right*, interior.

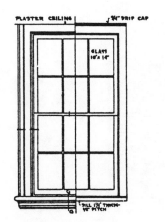

First-floor window elevation:
left, interior; *right*, exterior.

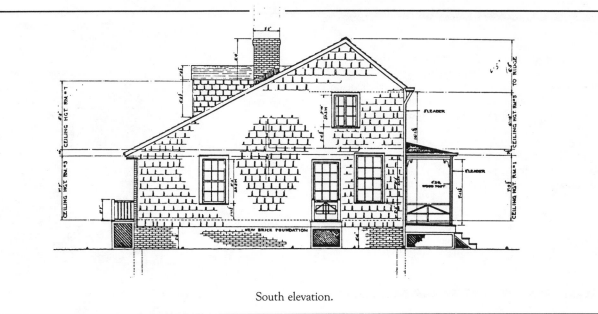

South elevation.

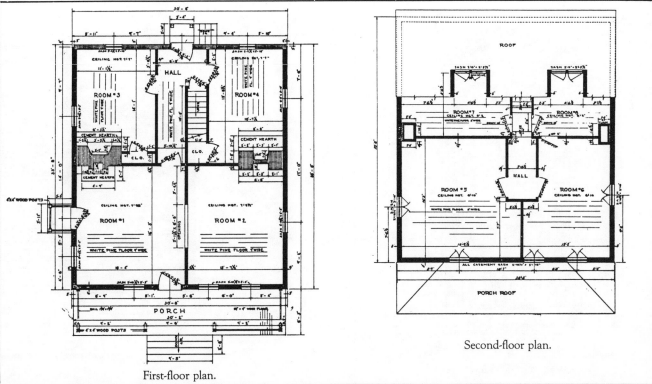

First-floor plan.

Second-floor plan.

24. **Scull-Humphreys House**, Auburn, New Jersey, c. 1790; frame addition, 1800. Although wedded stylistically, the two sections of this dwelling appear from the outside to be separate town houses. The smaller brick building is the older. Inside, the communication between the two sections is minimal, but enough to suggest that this was a one-family dwelling and not intended for two. The use of an ornate entrance leaves little doubt but that one should enter the building at the left and not through the modestly scaled doorway to the right.

The enlarged building has four chimneys, the two in front serving six fireplaces on the first and second floors. The chimneys at the right rear of the original section were for venting cooking fires. The first-floor plan (p. 62) shows that this room originally had a large cooking fireplace and oven, as well as a differently placed set of stairs.

Southeast (front) elevation.

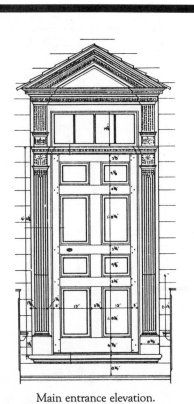

Main entrance elevation.

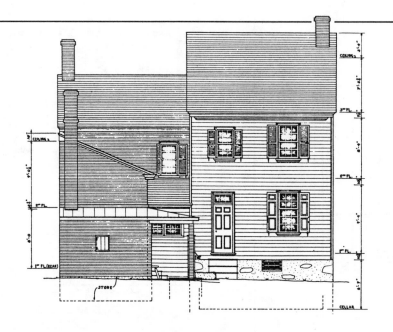

Northwest elevation.

Northeast elevation.

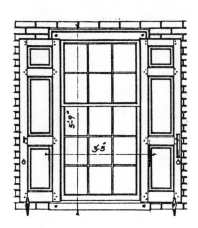

First-floor front window elevation, exterior, brick section.

Southwest elevation.

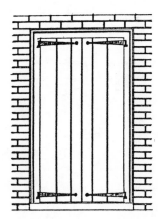

First-floor window elevation with shutters closed, brick section.

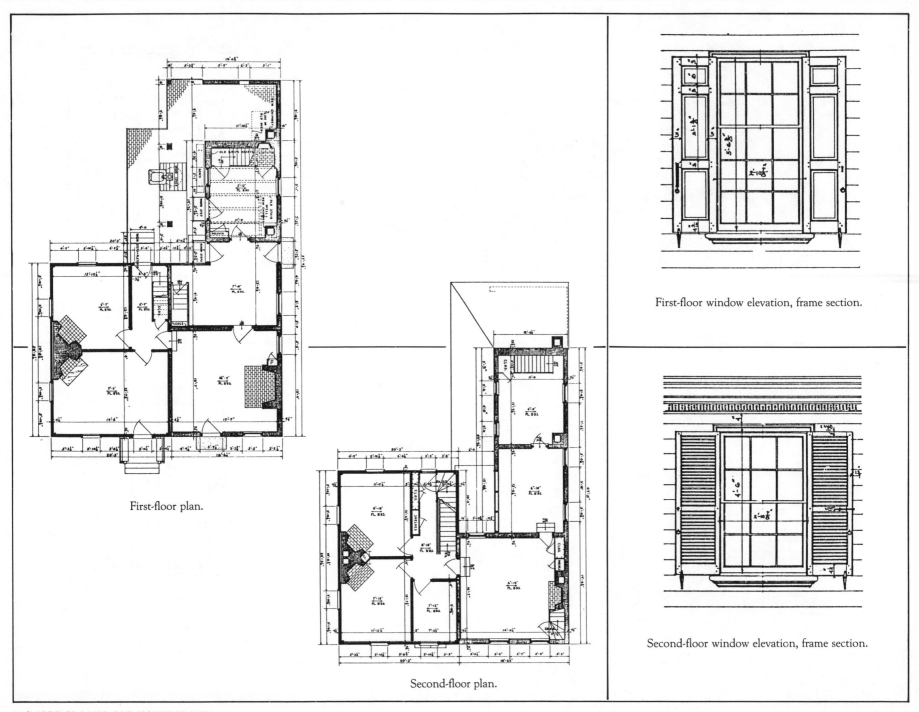

First-floor plan.

Second-floor plan.

First-floor window elevation, frame section.

Second-floor window elevation, frame section.

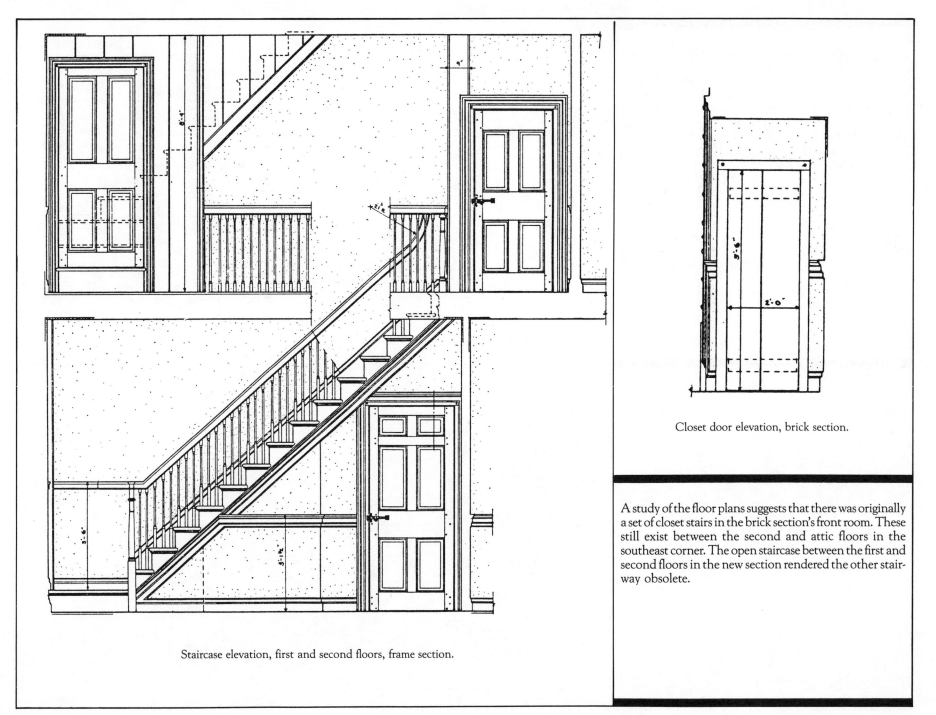

Staircase elevation, first and second floors, frame section.

Closet door elevation, brick section.

A study of the floor plans suggests that there was originally a set of closet stairs in the brick section's front room. These still exist between the second and attic floors in the southeast corner. The open staircase between the first and second floors in the new section rendered the other stairway obsolete.

25. Schenck-Polhemus House, Bridgewater, New Jersey, 1803-10. A side-hall Colonial with an el, this farmhouse is as practically laid out as it is handsomely designed. Off the wide hall in the main block are a square living room and a sitting room, each of which is served by a center chimney. In the el to the other side of the hall is a dining room and kitchen, the latter containing a massive cooking fireplace. Three bedrooms, two of them with fireplaces, are located on the second floor of the main section; the lower el contains only attic storage space.

The sash shown here are the original ones found on the property and incorporated by the draftsman. The small windows to each side of the main entrance are not original. Both the front and rear porch, however, appear to be part of the original design. Three sides of the building's main section have clapboard siding, some of which is original. The fourth wall has later wood shingling. Two of the sides of the el are covered with their original clapboards.

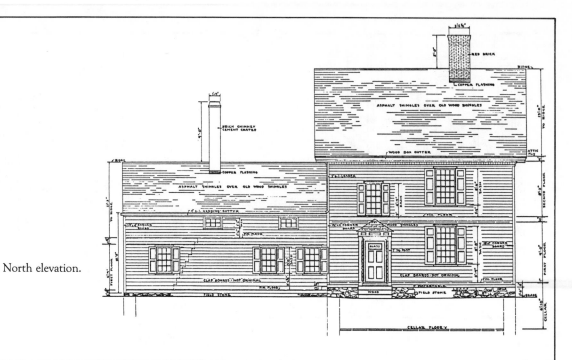

North elevation.

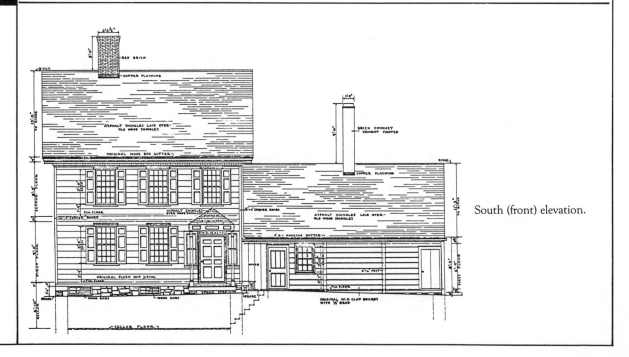

South (front) elevation.

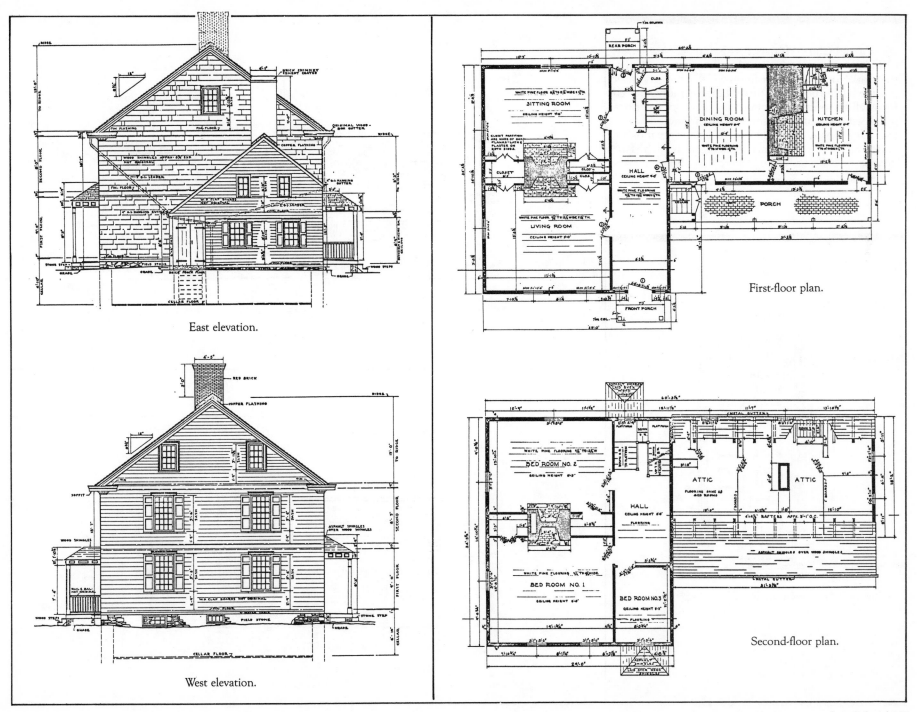

East elevation.

West elevation.

First-floor plan.

Second-floor plan.

26. **Adrial Clark House**, Port Republic, New Jersey, c. 1812-14, with later addition. A strikingly simple design, the Clark House was originally only 22′4″ x 15′5″, the taller portion having been built first. The dimensions allowed for a hall and one large room on the first floor and three small bedrooms on the second. With the addition came four more rooms. Dotted lines on the drawings indicate parts which are not original to either section, such as the doorway in the new section. There have also been additions to the rear.

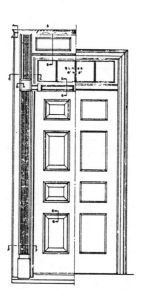

Main entrance elevation: *left*, exterior; *right*, interior.

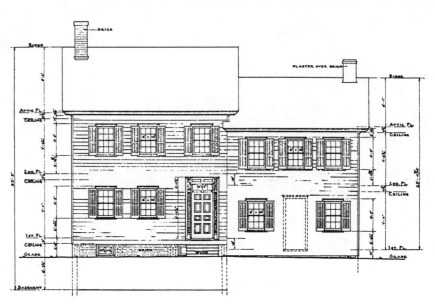

South (front) elevation.

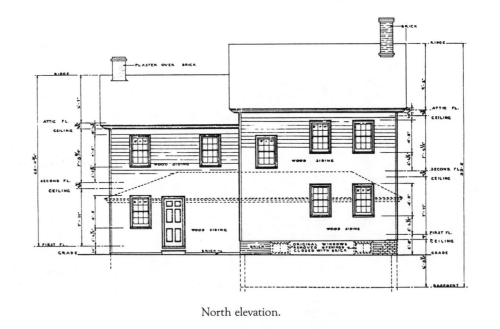

North elevation.

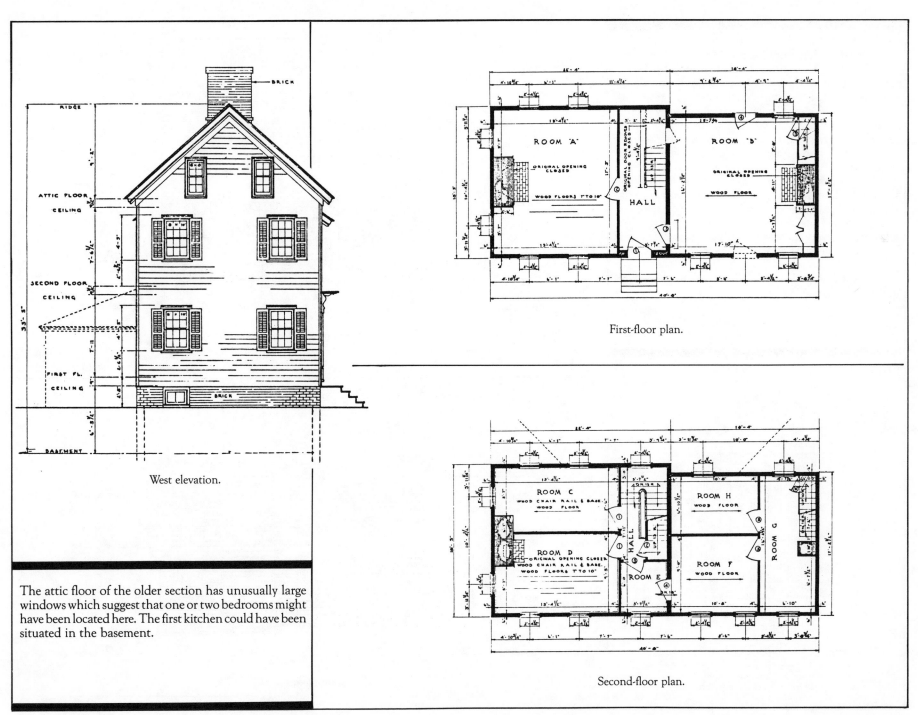

West elevation.

First-floor plan.

Second-floor plan.

The attic floor of the older section has unusually large windows which suggest that one or two bedrooms might have been located here. The first kitchen could have been situated in the basement.

27. Charles Lighthipe House, Orange, New Jersey, 1808-28. In what stages this house came together is not known, but it is clear that a pleasing overall design emerged. The use of cornice brackets and a dormer with pointed-arch windows anticipates elements of Victorian style. The main entrance with its portico, sidelights, and fanlight, and the stylized window brackets of the main section, reflect an appreciation for the then-popular Federal style.

Inside the house a similar mix of styles prevails. Doorways and windows are trimmed with either corner blocks and fluted moldings or simpler molding assemblies. Sliding doors divide the sitting room from the parlor. The gracefully curved main stairway has a newel, rail, and balusters of mahogany and treads, risers, and trim of white pine.

All of the principal rooms are furnished with fireplaces and paneled wood mantels.

North (front) elevation.

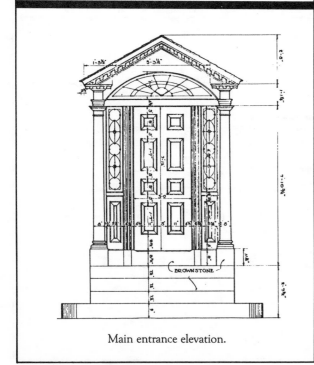

Main entrance elevation.

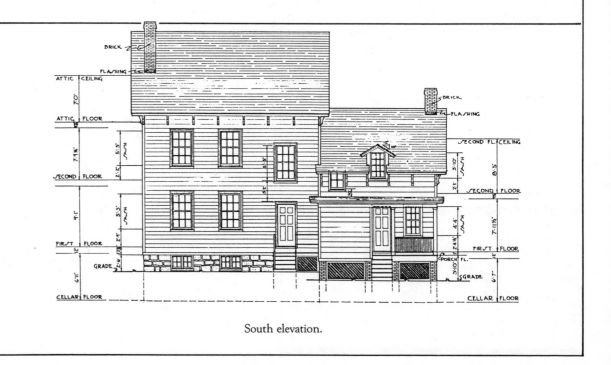

South elevation.

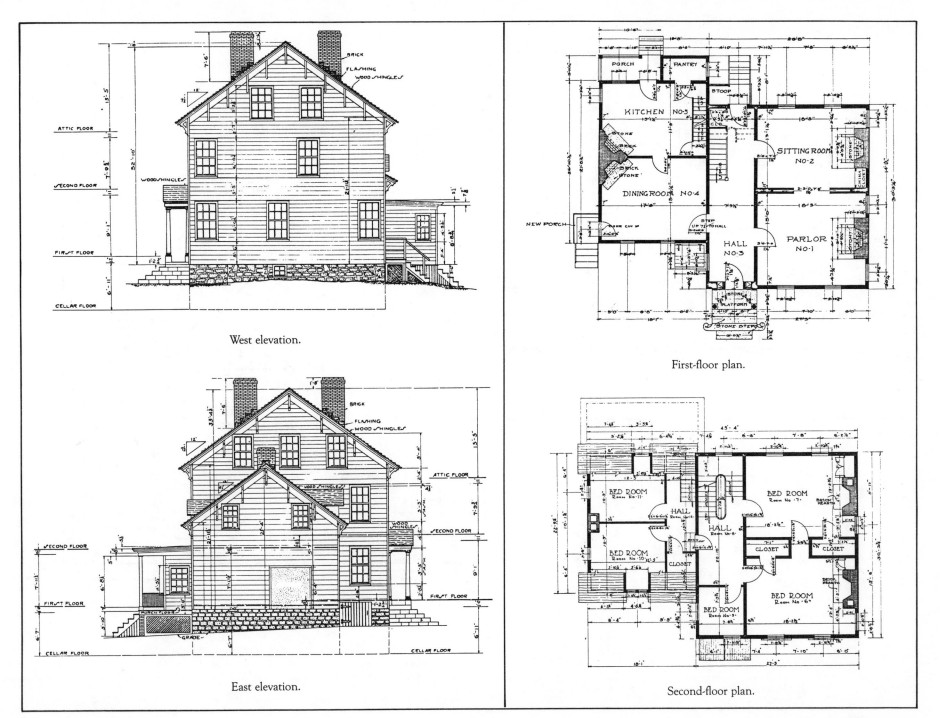

West elevation.

First-floor plan.

East elevation.

Second-floor plan.

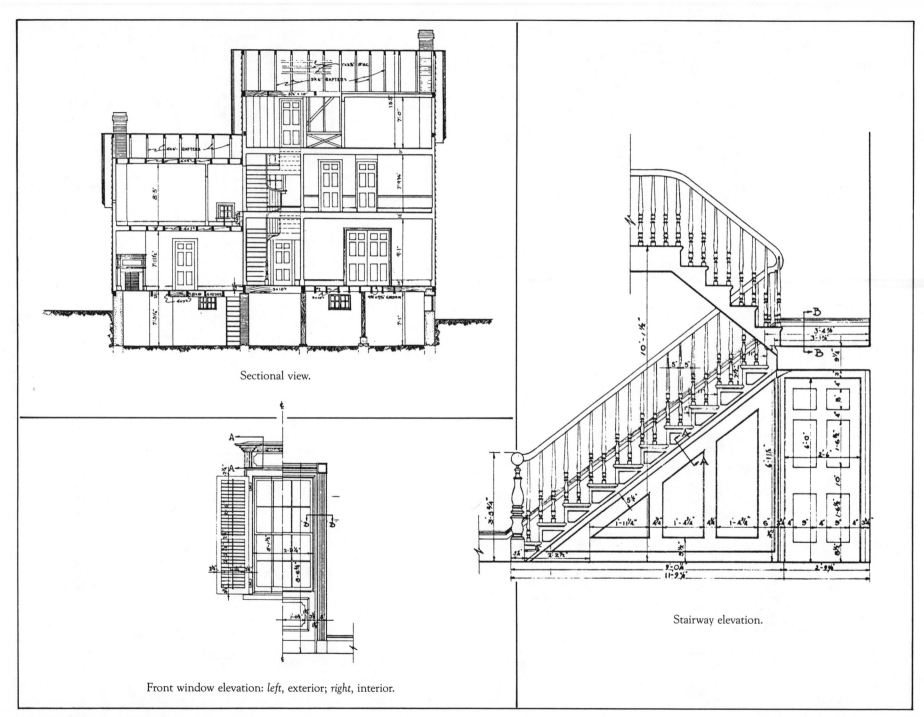

Sectional view.

Front window elevation: *left*, exterior; *right*, interior.

Stairway elevation.

Victorian Home Plans

Early Victorian

The turn to romantic forms of architecture which we now call Victorian was well underway in America before Victoria ascended the British throne in 1837. Since the second decade of the 19th century, proponents of the Gothic Revival and Greek Revival building styles were proselytizing for buildings more picturesque in form and decoration than the Colonial. The Gothic pointed arch, the neo-classical portico, cross gables, window bays—these and other architectural elements rarely seen for generations were increasingly used in domestic architecture. The change in taste in most areas of the country, however, was slow, taken in small steps even by the most *au courant* arbiters of architectural fashion. The symmetrical center-hall floor plan found in most Colonial homes persisted in use along with the newer side-hall arrangement of rooms. When change was adopted, it was more sober and formal and much less asymmetrical in composition than that adopted later in the century.

The Greek Revival is a transitional style both looking back to Georgian Colonial and Federal precedents and forward to full antebellum romanticism. One of the most popular building styles of the 19th century, the Greek Revival was favored for both public buildings and residences. Its essential neo-classical spirit was aesthetically in tune with the symbols and rhetoric of the early democratic republic of free citizens. A classical order of columns framed a temple-form building and gave it stature and flair. Where a portico was not used, pilasters, sometimes projecting, defined a façade. And, almost always, there was an imposing entrance consisting of pediments, sidelights, transom, and architrave or lintel. Other typical Greek Revival decorative elements sometimes incorporated on both the exterior and interior of a house were dentil moldings, friezes, and panels with stylized acanthus leaves or anthemion ornaments.

The Gothic Revival is more recognizably Victorian in form to our modern sensibility. Its angular proportions, vaulted spaces, and fanciful ornaments were found to be perfectly in tune with the needs of liturgically-minded churches and church-related institutions in the early Victorian era. The style was frequently adopted for Episcopal and Roman Catholic church buildings. In pure form, however, the Gothic style was never widely adopted by Americans for domestic buildings. What eventually emerged on the American scene as a picturesque alternative to the far more popular Greek Revival style was a vernacular variation. Gothic elements such as highly ornamental wood barge- or vergeboards covered gables; board-and-batten siding was substituted for horizontal clapboards; a pointed-arch window was placed in a cross gable.

28. Watkins-Coleman House, Midway, Utah, c. 1868, built by John C. Watkins. This basic Gothic Revival town residence was designed by its first owner, but it could have been copied from plans by A. J. Downing or his followers. Many of the essential features of the style—gable fenestration, pointed-arch windows, roof finials, pediment-shaped window heads, and a fanciful verandah—are found in this spacious 46' x 41'6" house. Only the use of adobe brick, painted red, and sandstone quoins distinguishes the house from Eastern prototypes. From the front, the building appears larger than it actually is. The two side gable wings extend back only twenty feet. As shown on the main floor plan, the original kitchen was located behind the left wing; on the right was an open porch (now the kitchen and pantry). On the second floor are three bedrooms, all situated over the building's front section; the space above the rear parlor is devoted to storage.

First-floor bedrooms are often found in 18th- and 19th-century homes, and two such rooms are provided here. Each is supplied with a fireplace, as are the second-floor bedrooms. Fireplaces are also located in the front and rear parlors. Indoor plumbing was absent, a bathroom having been cut out of the rear parlor space at a later date.

South (front) elevation.

First-floor plan.

Second-floor plan.

29. **James D. Roberts House**, Carson City, Nevada, 1859. Originally located in Washoe City, this handsome wood-frame house was moved on a railroad flatcar in 1873 to its new site. A modest workingman's cottage, it was designed with considerable taste in the Gothic Revival style. The side entrance projects four feet from the rectangular main block and is composed of Gothic sidelights, paneled doors, and a simple transom; above this is an extended balcony which frames an impressive arched portal. Decorative bargeboards outline the side gable and the west gable end. The simpler main entrance is handsomely set off by a three-bay verandah.

The floor plan is simplicity itself, with two side parlors and a bathroom on the first floor and two bedrooms and a bath on the second. What is now the second-floor bath was probably originally a sewing room. Just where the kitchen was located is unknown; logically, it would have been situated in the left rear first-floor space now designated a bedroom.

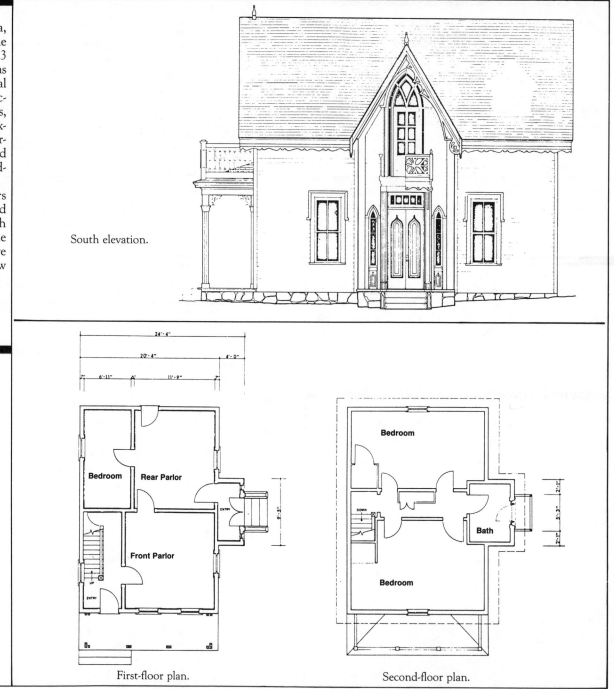

South elevation.

First-floor plan.

Second-floor plan.

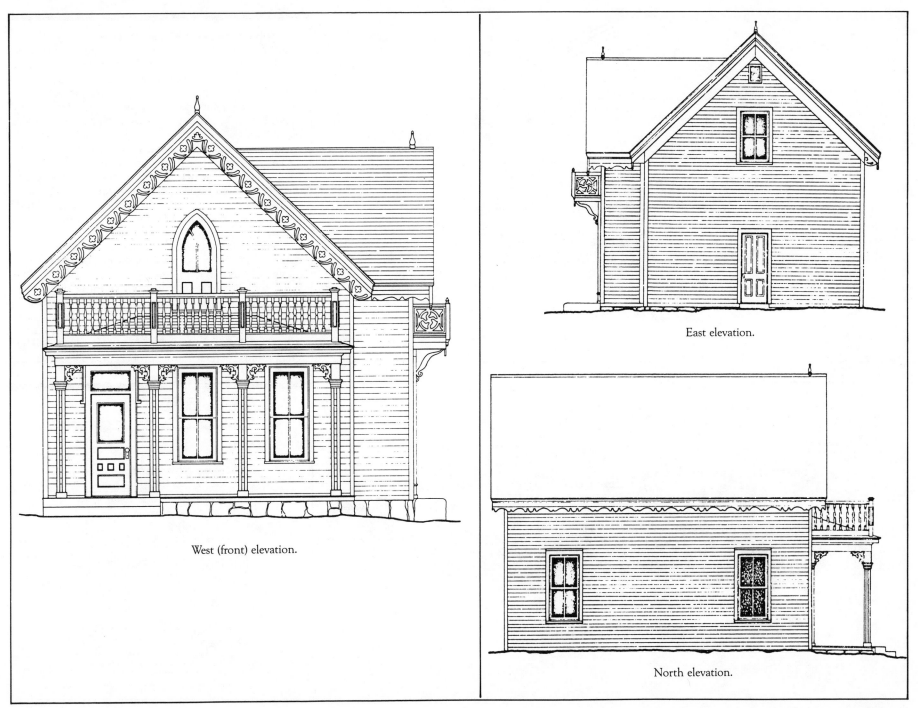

West (front) elevation.

East elevation.

North elevation.

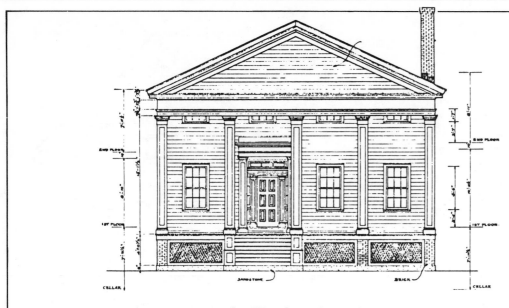

West (front) elevation.

30. **John Van Brunt House**, Englewood, New Jersey, 1834. The neo-classical forms and decorative features which define the Greek Revival style are graphically in evidence both inside and outside the frame Van Brunt house. The 36'-wide portico with plain square wood columns is of a type found throughout the United States. The main entrance is typical, too, of the Greek Revival house, being a well-proportioned assembly consisting of a cornice, architrave, pediments, sidelights, and transom. Other representative exterior features are the raking gable cornice and the use of eyebrow windows at the second-floor level. Inside, doors and windows are defined by neo-classical trim, mantels are composed of pediments and an architrave, and moldings in the first-floor formal rooms include dentil and egg-and-dart forms.

The first-floor room layout is determined by a central hall plan. Four rooms, including two adjoining parlors (designated as a living room and a dining room on the floor plan), are located in the front building block. The rear extension includes the present kitchen (probably once the dining room) and the original kitchen, now a bathroom. The second-floor bedroom level is reached by a center stairway; no back set of stairs is indicated. The small rooms to the rear were probably used by servants.

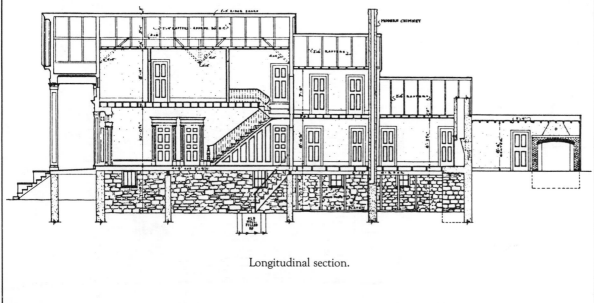

Longitudinal section.

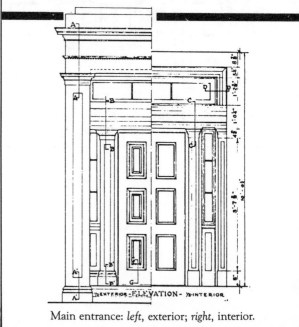

Main entrance: *left*, exterior; *right*, interior.

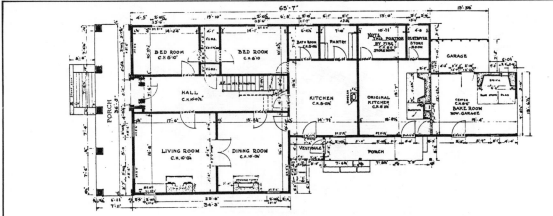

First-floor plan.

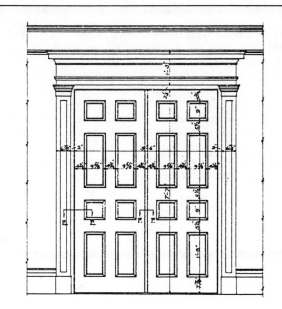

Pocket doors, parlor, elevation.

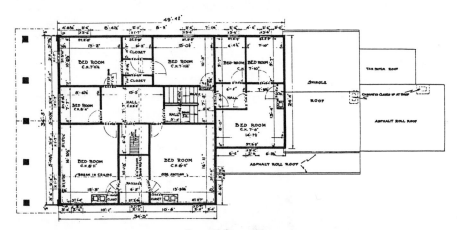

Second-floor plan.

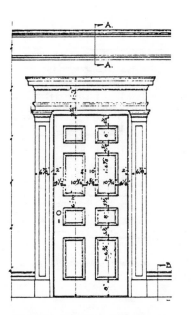

Typical interior door elevation.

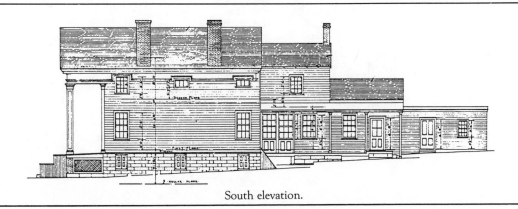

South elevation.

31. **Colonel Warren Residence**, Warrenville, Illinois, 1834-35. Similar to the Federal houses which preceded them in popularity, many Greek Revival residences were designed with a side hall plan. This early and quite typical Midwestern Greek Revival residence consists of a two-story 20′2″ x 26′2″ box to which a side shed and a rear extension were added. All three sections appear to have been built at approximately the same time. The broad raking gable cornice with returns at the eaves is accented with dentils. The main entrance is typical of those found in Greek Revival houses.

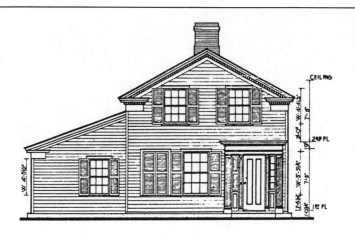

South (front) elevation.

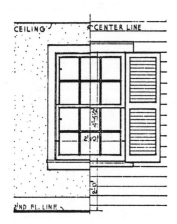

Second-floor window elevation: *left*, inside; *right*, outside.

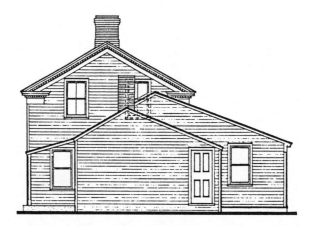

North elevation.

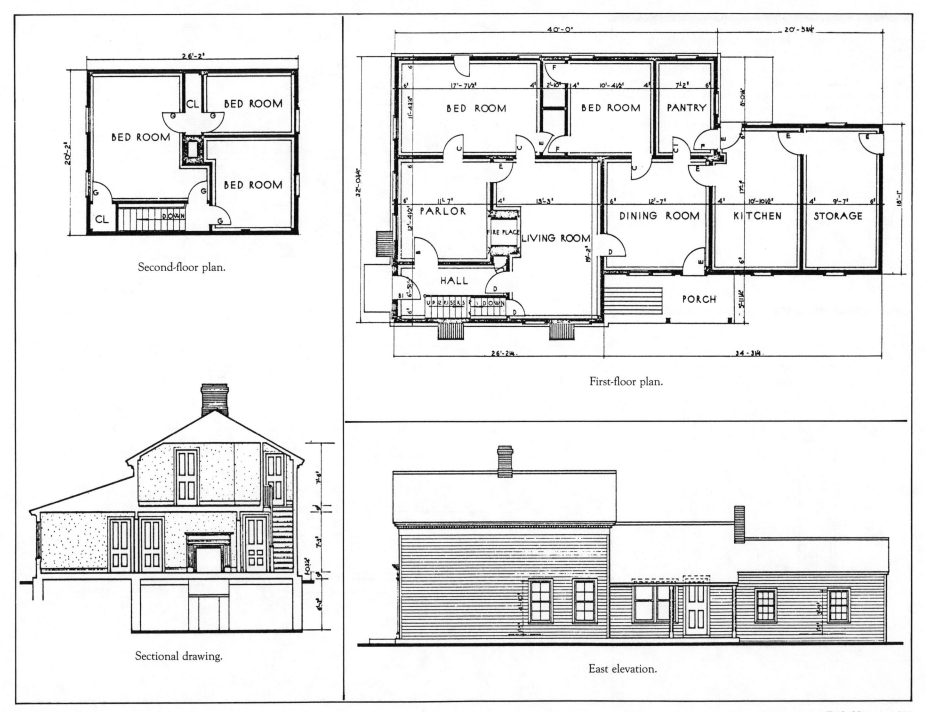

Second-floor plan.

First-floor plan.

Sectional drawing.

East elevation.

32. **Major Aaron Hudson House**, Mendham, New Jersey, c. 1842, Maj. Hudson the probable architect. A true Greek Revival mansion, the Hudson dwelling could serve as a much better model for a prestigious columned residence than many modern versions. The two-story, 16′9″-high central projecting pavilion is what gives the building its air of monumentality. The front first-floor reception rooms are 9′6″ from floor to ceiling and have long 9-over-6 windows. The curious ogee window over the typical Greek Revival entrance is not original; what was formerly here is unknown.

Later in the 19th century, the first floor was extended to the rear; dotted lines on the floor plan indicate the additions. The second-floor plan gives a better indication of the original dimensions.

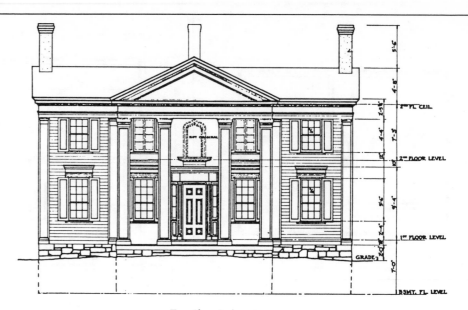

East (front) elevation.

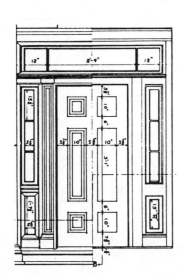

Main entrance elevation: *left*, exterior; *right*, interior.

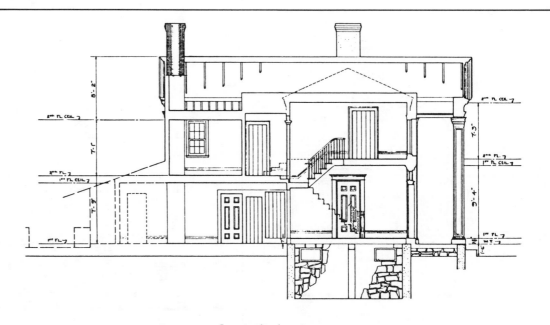

Longitudinal section.

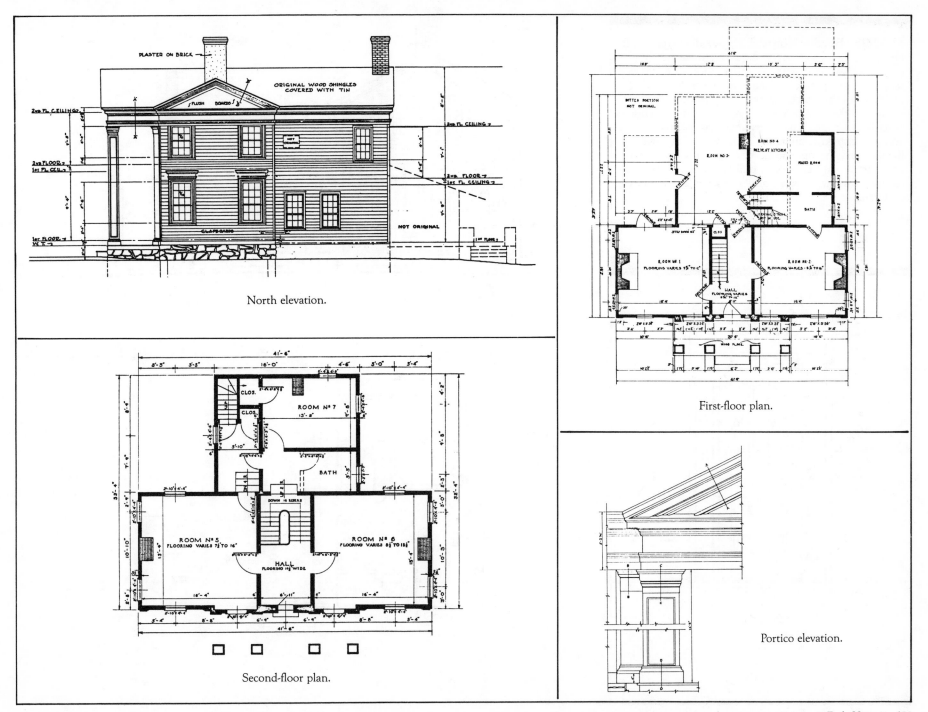

North elevation.

First-floor plan.

Second-floor plan.

Portico elevation.

33. Mike Bender House, Bloomingdale vicinity, Illinois, c. 1850. A modest farmhouse distinguished by fine Greek Revival detailing, the Bender residence could well serve as a good prototype for a modern one-family dwelling. Built in three sections, the two in front earlier than the rear el, the house offers four bedrooms and adequate space for such modern improvements as bathrooms and an up-to-date kitchen which make an historic dwelling livable today. Among the most handsome features of this wood frame and clapboard building are the main entrance, columned porch, and the interior door and window trim—all elements illustrated here.

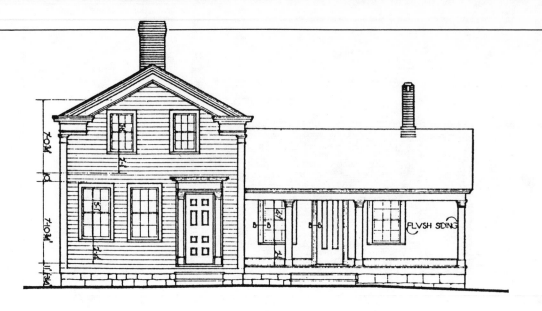

South (front) elevation.

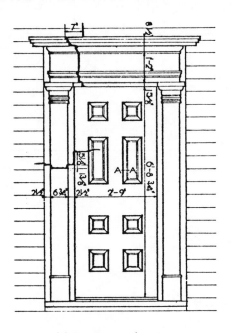

Main entrance elevation.

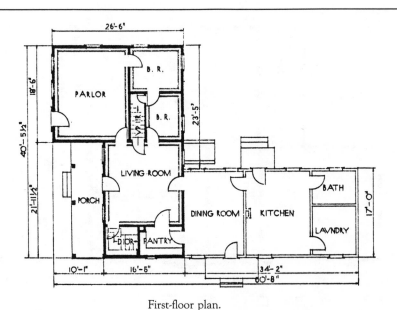

First-floor plan.

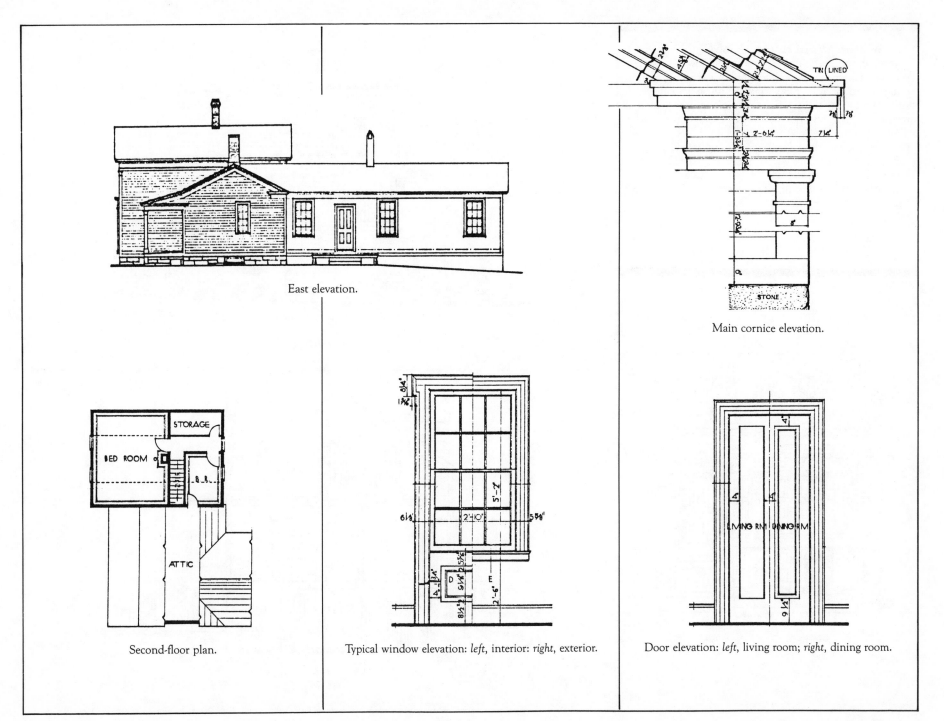

East elevation.

Main cornice elevation.

Second-floor plan.

Typical window elevation: *left*, interior: *right*, exterior.

Door elevation: *left*, living room; *right*, dining room.

34. William Alcorn House, Union City, New Jersey, c. 1846. A two-and-a-half story side-hall town house, the Alcorn residence offers an ideal plan for a building on a narrow town or city lot. Maximum use is made of all space, including the top floor where dormers—original to the building, and not awkwardly tacked on at a later date—open up the space to air and light. As was often the case in such urban dwellings, functions such as cooking, bathing, and dining were allocated to the lowest or basement level. The main floor now includes an adjoining parlor and bedroom; originally the space may have been intended for a double parlor.

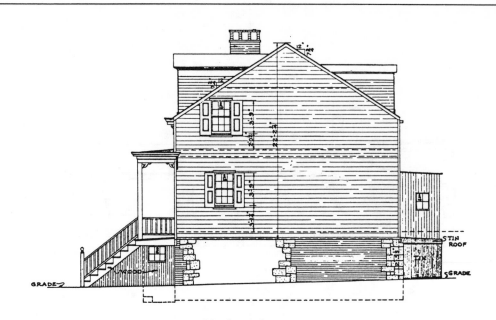

Northeast elevation.

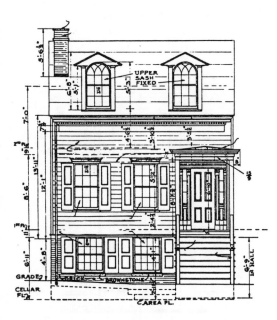

Southeast (front) elevation.

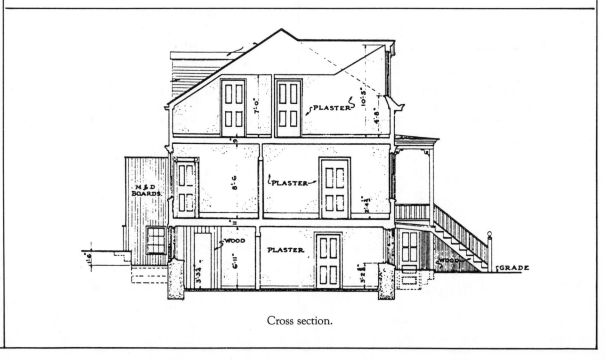

Cross section.

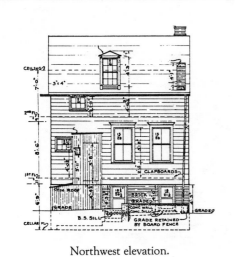

Northwest elevation.

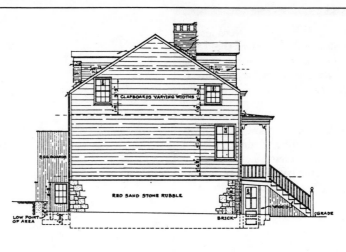

Southwest elevation.

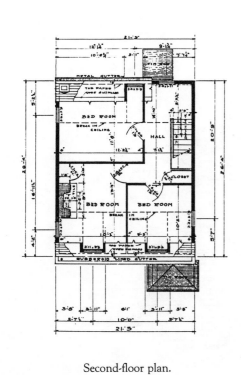

Second-floor plan.

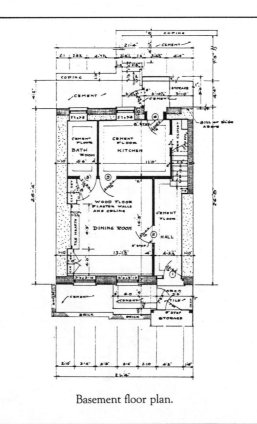

Basement floor plan.

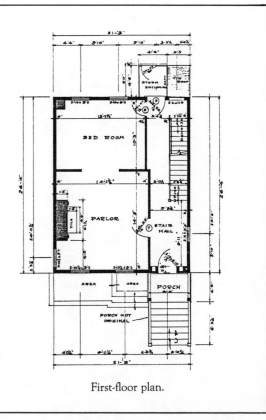

First-floor plan.

35. Reading-Large House, Flemington, New Jersey, c. 1854, designed by Mahlon Fisher. One of the finest Greek Revival houses in the country, this residence was one of several designed by a gifted country architect-builder in the seat of Hunterdon County. The splendid Ionic portico, bracketed cornice, roof cresting, and cupola set the building's stylish tone. Inside, the door and window trim is similarly detailed. As in many other town residences of the period, the cooking and serving of food was reserved for the half-basement level. Later, a dining room was incorporated on the main floor. The bedrooms on the attic floor were reserved for household help.

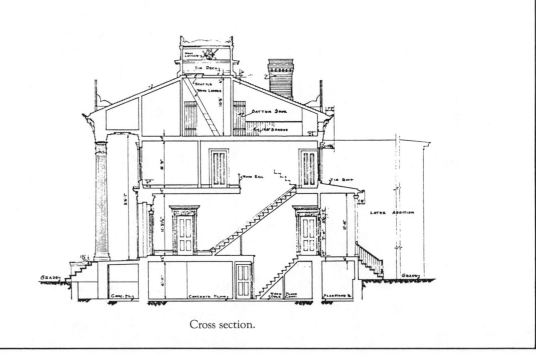

East (front) elevation.

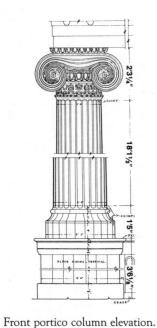

Front portico column elevation.

Cross section.

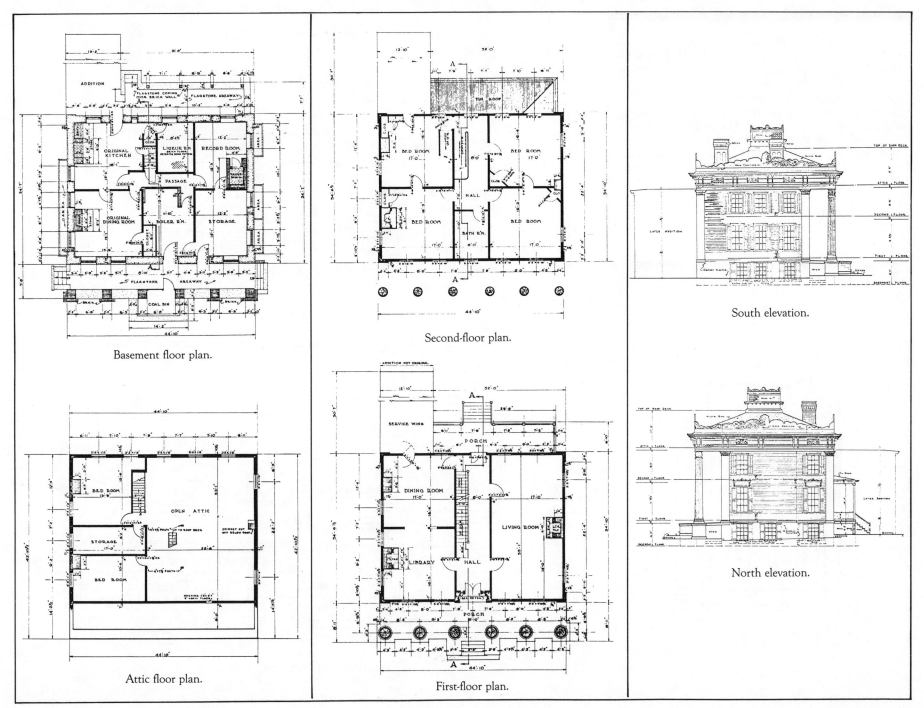

Basement floor plan.

Second-floor plan.

South elevation.

Attic floor plan.

First-floor plan.

North elevation.

36. **Joel O. Magie House**, Elizabeth, New Jersey, c. 1850. A center-hall building, this residence was efficiently and imaginatively laid out to provide ample but conveniently arranged living space in each of the structure's four quarters. The eyebrow windows across the second-floor front and dormers at the rear are attractive and practical features. The typical Greek Revival entrance and adjoining side porch complement each other. A bathroom has been provided on the second floor, and another such room easily could be incorporated on the first floor.

Southeast (front) elevation.

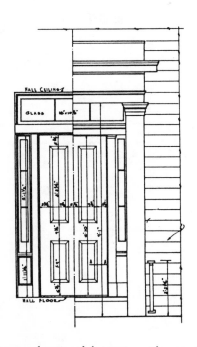

Entrance elevation: *left,* interior; *right,* exterior.

Northwest elevation.

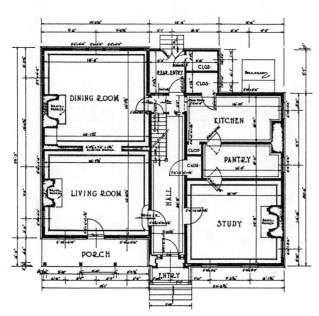

First-floor plan.

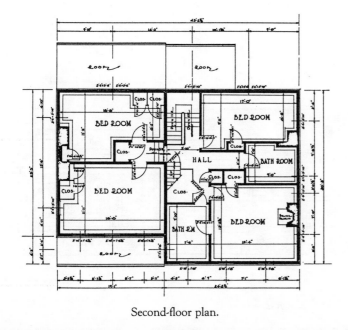

Second-floor plan.

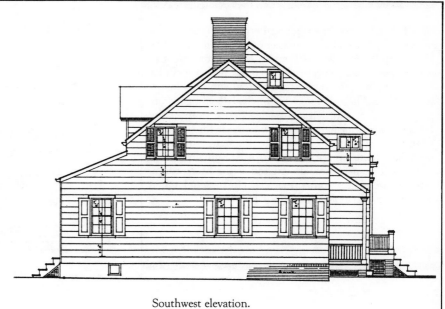

Southwest elevation.

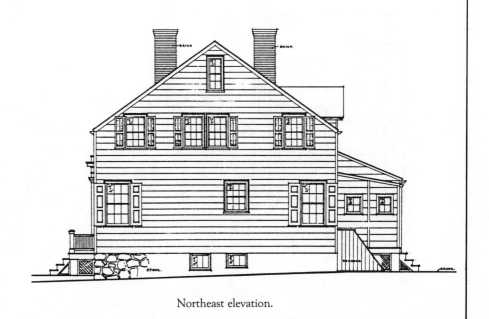

Northeast elevation.

37. Elihu Wilcox House, Elizabeth, New Jersey, 1850, designed by Brandt Crane, master builder. Like the Magie House (pp. 92-93), also in Elizabeth, the Wilcox residence was designed as a center-hall dwelling. It also includes a side wing with a porch and eyebrow windows below the roof line. The exterior Greek Revival detailing is more pronounced on this substantial residence than in the former house. Special provision was made for the work of servants in the side wing. The kitchen, with a formidable cooking fireplace and oven, was originally located in this wing, space now designated as the living room. Above it were the servants' quarters. The present kitchen was once a convenient first-floor bedroom.

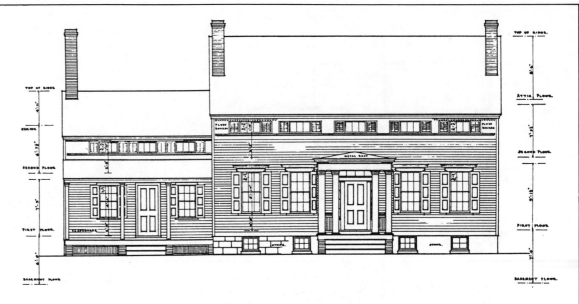

North (front) elevation.

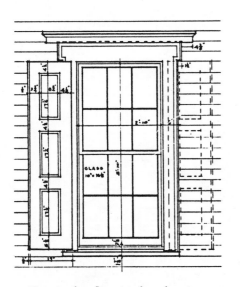

Exterior first-floor window elevation.

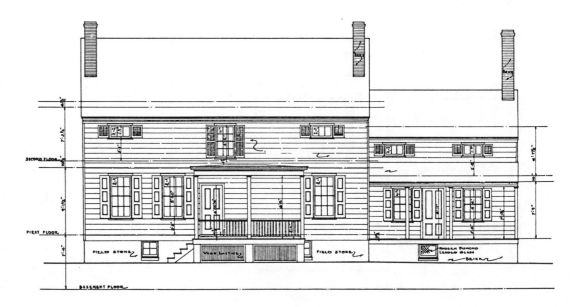

South elevation.

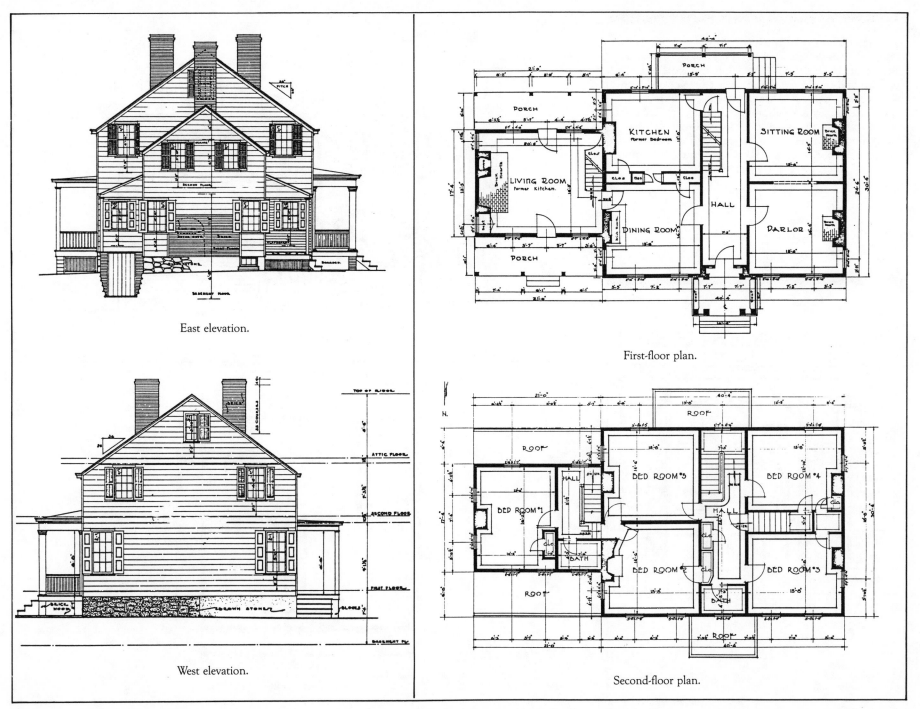

East elevation.

First-floor plan.

West elevation.

Second-floor plan.

38. John Hancock House, Bentonsport, Iowa, 1850s, built by James Brown. A two-story rectangle with a one-story el at the rear, the Hancock house is representative of many mid-century Midwestern dwellings. Wood frame with clapboards and a heavily bracketed cornice, it is distinguished by an elaborate entrance, the design of which extends to the second story. Only the finest building materials were used throughout, including black walnut clapboard siding, black walnut and oak flooring, and black walnut mantels. The metal roofing is a typical feature.

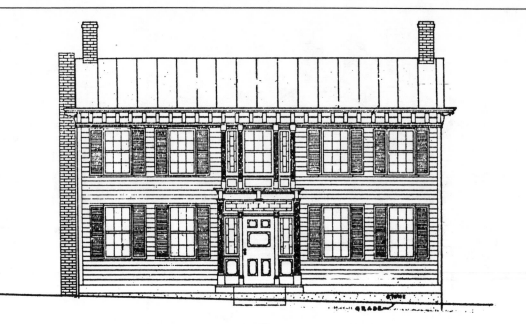

West (front) elevation.

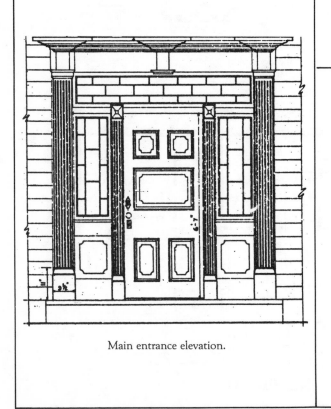

Main entrance elevation.

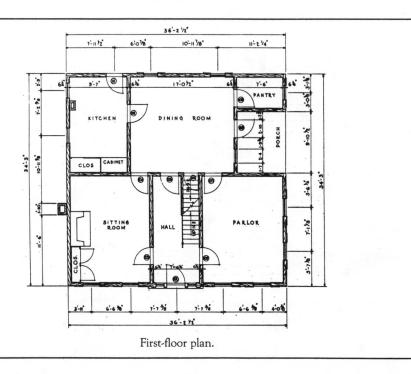

First-floor plan.

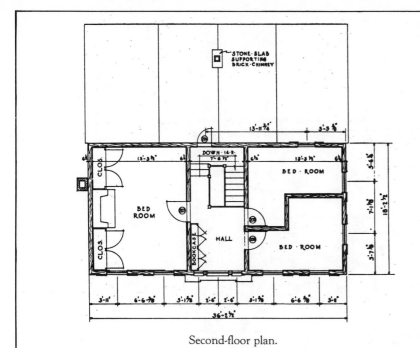

Second-floor plan.

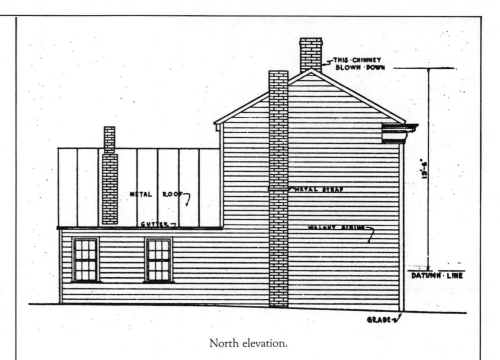

North elevation.

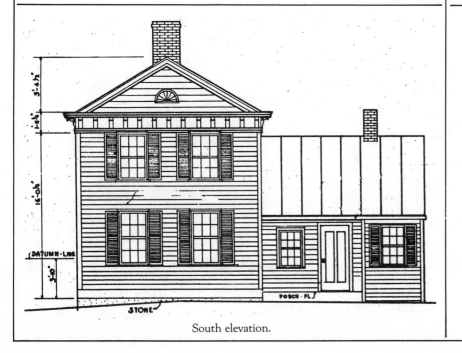

South elevation.

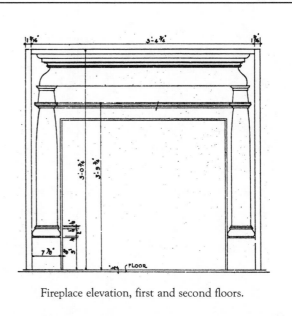

Fireplace elevation, first and second floors.

39. **General Ulysses S. Grant House**, Galena, Illinois, 1859. The first Galena house owned by the Civil War hero and later President was a handsome and modest dwelling place. A front porch, added later, is not shown. Designed as a side-hall residence, it features a typical double parlor, one room of which is now designated as a dining room. A wood-frame kitchen wing once extended at the rear. The simple red-brick residence has a metal roof with a generous overhang; each window is fitted with louvered shutters. The entrance is a typical Greek Revival arrangement with sidelights and transom. A curved front hall, which allows for a graceful stairway, distinguishes the interior. Three bedrooms are located on the second floor.

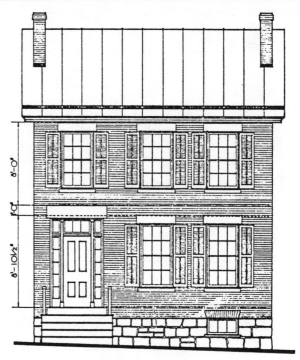

East (front) elevation.

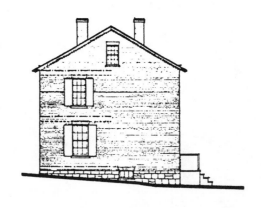

South elevation.

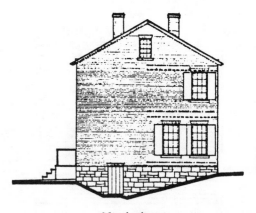

North elevation.

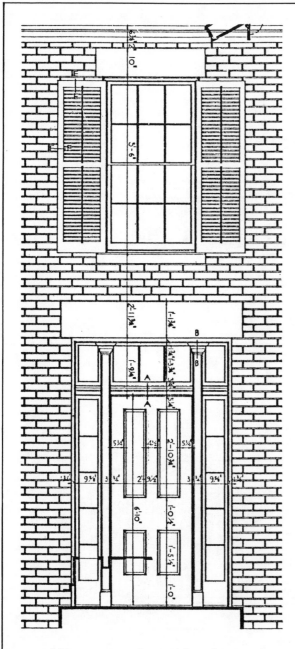

Main entrance and second-floor elevation.

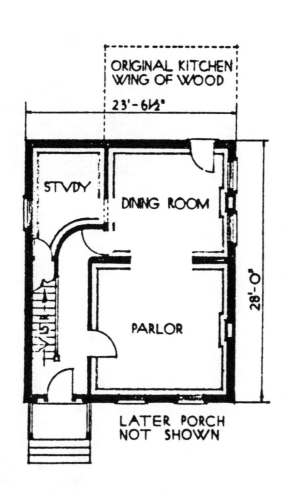

ORIGINAL KITCHEN
WING OF WOOD

23'-6½"

STUDY

DINING ROOM

PARLOR

28'-0"

LATER PORCH
NOT SHOWN

First-floor plan.

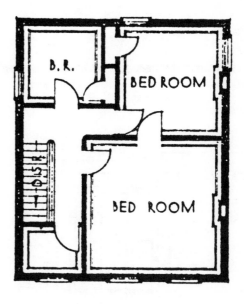

B.R.

BED ROOM

BED ROOM

Second-floor plan.

40. **Dr. James K. Lewis House**, St. Charles, Illinois, 1859, Dr. James K. Lewis, builder. Typical of Greek Revival homes built by New England settlers in western New York and the Midwest, the Lewis residence grew over the years. The original building is a temple-form rectangle, the two side wings having been added slightly later. The two-tier portico, the rear bay window of the original section, and the shouldered exterior and interior framing of the windows and doors are testimony to the builder's fine mastery of Greek Revival form and detailing.

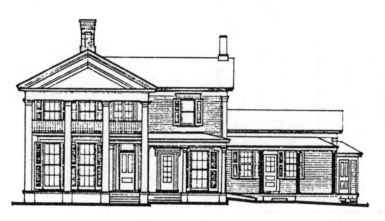

East (front) elevation.

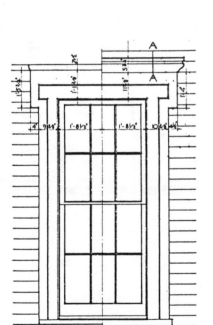

Exterior living room window elevation: *left*, porch; *right*, south wall.

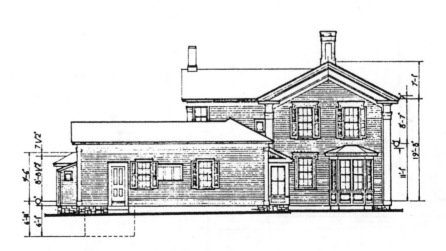

West elevation.

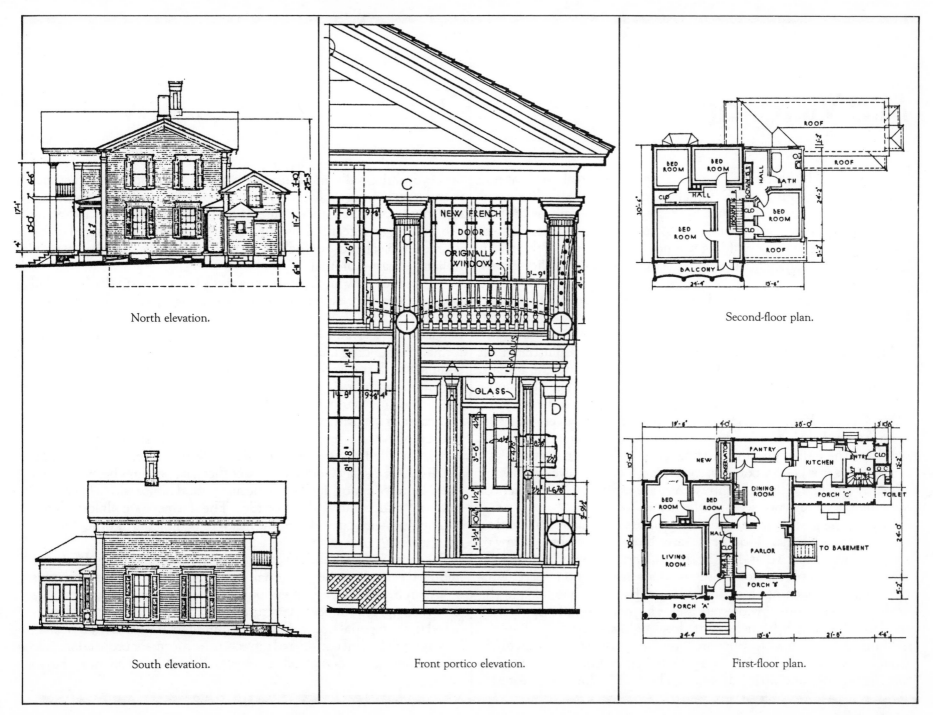

North elevation.

South elevation.

Front portico elevation.

NEW FRENCH DOOR ORIGINALLY WINDOW

GLASS

Second-floor plan.

BED ROOM

BED ROOM

CLO

HALL

HALL

BATH

BED ROOM

BED ROOM

ROOF

ROOF

ROOF

BALCONY

First-floor plan.

NEW

PANTRY

DINING ROOM

KITCHEN

ENTRY

CLO

BED ROOM

BED ROOM

PORCH 'C'

TOILET

LIVING ROOM

HALL

CLO

PARLOR

TO BASEMENT

PORCH 'B'

PORCH 'A'

Mid-Victorian

The typical mid-19th century house is what many real estate agents describe in their listings as "Colonial." Although there is added commercial value to the use of the anachronistic term, especially on the East Coast, these purveyors of property are correct in some respects. Despite the fact that this type of building was not erected in the 17th or 18th centuries, it does share many stylistic features with the earlier form—rectilinear lines, a symmetrical arrangement of doors and windows, the use of exterior shutters, paneled doors, and multipane window sash. Only with closer study does the true character of the mid-Victorian home emerge.

The vernacular or popular house of the period is illustrated on pp. 101-105. Both the Grover Cleveland Birthplace and the Minard Coeyman House display features distinctive of the era. The most noticeable is the roof line, broken by either a projecting gable or a cross gable. Centered in the gable is a small arched window very different from the windows in the floors below. In the Cleveland house, the roofs overhang the wall limits, and provide space for boxed-in gutters. Both houses have front entry porches, the typical Colonial dwelling having none at all. The Cleveland house has an additional side porch or verandah, a feature not seen until the mid-1800s.

In scale the mid-Victorian house is considerably larger than either the common Colonial model or an early 19th-century home. Many of these homes are of two-and-a-half stories, and the top or attic floor is designed not simply for storage but as additional bedroom space. Window and door openings are usually larger than they had been in the 18th century; an open, wide staircase or a straight set of steps is used in place of an old-fashioned set of closet tightwinders.

Many of these "new" features are found in houses styled by architectural historians as Italianate. The pure Italianate house, however, is a large square or cube with side wings. The roof, of low pitch, extends far beyond the walls and is usually bracketed. A cupola is sometimes found atop the nearly flat roof. In most towns and villages, only a few stylistically pure Italianate houses were built by individuals following the latest in architectural fashion. What is usually encountered today is a more typical house of the 1840s which can only be described as part-Italianate, part-Colonial.

As America grew more prosperous and adventurous in the 1840s and '50s there was more experimentation in building style. The Joseph Staub House (pp. 106-107) is representative of a new departure in style, the Renaissance Revival, which became increasingly popular in large towns for narrow building lots. The style has a classic formality somewhat in common with the late-Colonial period, but the scale is larger and the appointments more irregular. The use of a two-story bay is typical; so, too, is the fancy cutout entry door surround.

Because of its distinctive and irregular roof line, the mansard or Second Empire home appears more Victorian in character. Still, many mansard-roofed houses, like the Robert Matches House of 1854-56 (pp. 108-109), display Colonial or early Victorian features below the roof line. Not uncommon at all is a Colonial-period house with a later mansard roof of decorative slates or tiles. The dormers are almost always accentuated with curved window heads or pediments or other form of decoration.

The most unusual and atypical of American building styles of the mid-19th century is the octagonal. Two examples of the design genius of Orson Squire Fowler, the popularizer of the eight-sided form, are shown on pp. 112-15. Because of its many exposures to light, Fowler believed the octagonal house more healthful than any other, and he may have been right. But considered too eccentric a form for proper domestic arrangements, the octagonal house was a short-lived phenomenon.

41. **Grover Cleveland Birthplace**, Caldwell, New Jersey, 1832. The Cleveland birthplace typifies a late-Colonial house Victorianized later in the 1800s. The original building consisted of no more than the left block and possibly the two-story one-room-deep el. (Differences in exterior clapboard siding and interior design suggest that the el may date somewhat later.) The fenestration was added to both the entrance and side porches later in the century. The front gable dormer is probably also a later addition. Cleveland's father, Richard, served as minister of the First Presbyterian Church, and the house was the manse.

West (front) elevation.

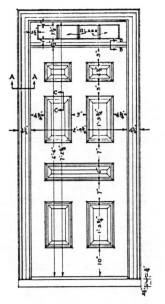

Front entrance elevation.

East elevation.

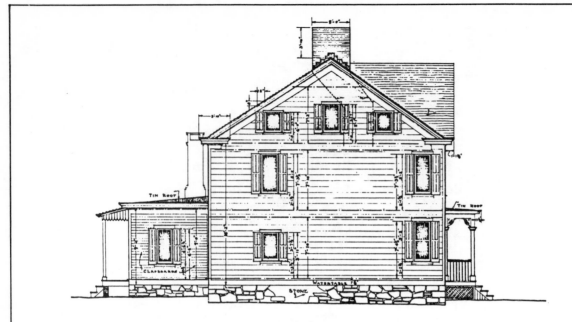

North elevation.

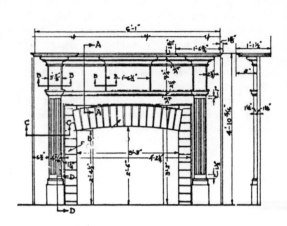

Living room fireplace elevation.

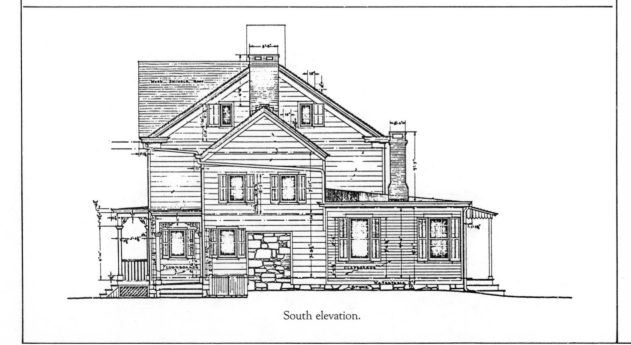

South elevation.

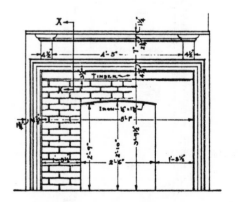

Dining room fireplace elevation.

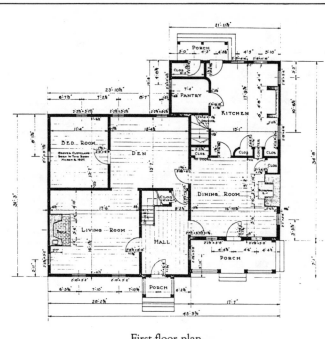

First-floor plan.

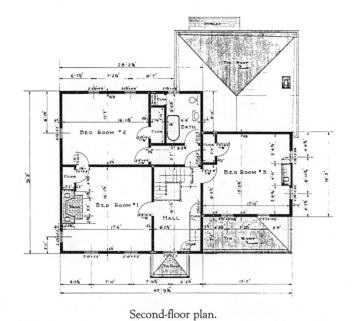

Second-floor plan.

Attic floor plan.

42. Minard Coeyman House, Belleville, New Jersey, c. 1850. The Coeyman residence is like many American houses, vernacular in style. It could be called Colonial by some because of its basic symmetrical lines, but some of the detailing is Victorian, in particular the bracketed cornice. The building is comfortably laid out, and a modern bathroom has been added on the first floor. As in many early homes, a bedroom has been provided on the first floor as well. The half-basement is well lighted and includes a laundry, storage room, and furnace room. The main entrance porch would appear to be a later addition.

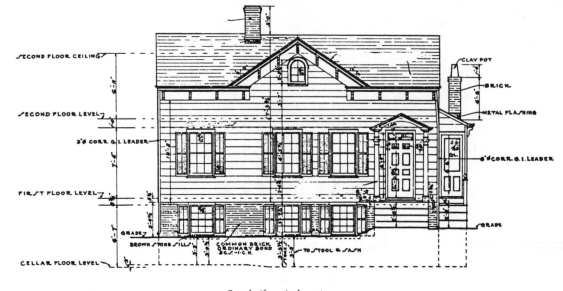

South (front) elevation.

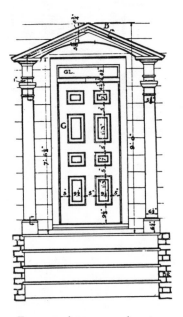

Front porch entrance elevation.

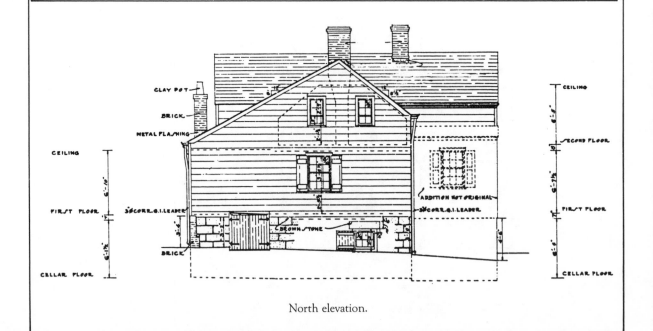

North elevation.

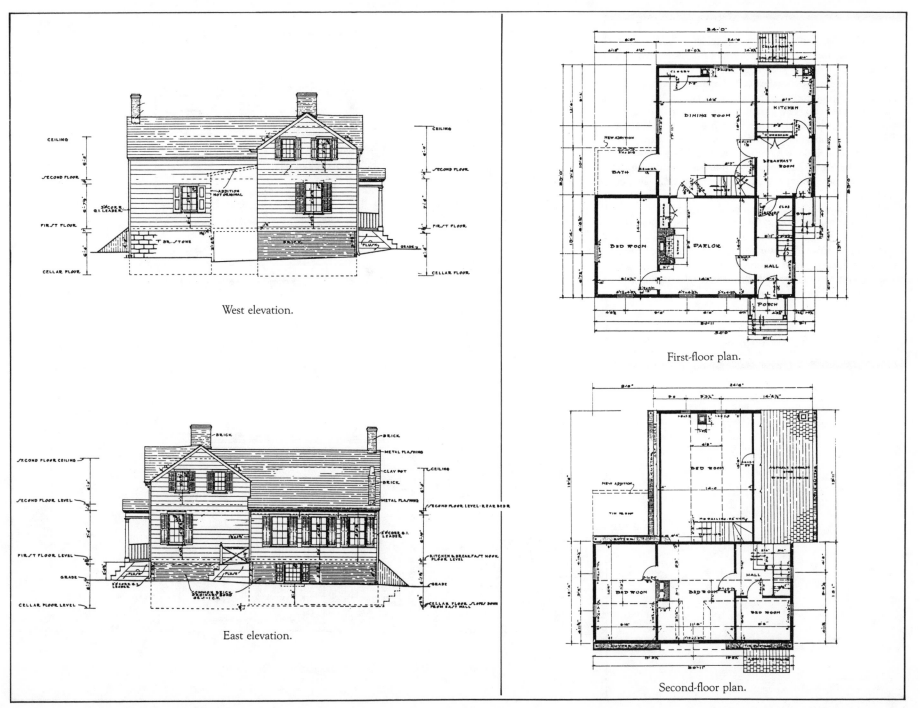

West elevation.

East elevation.

First-floor plan.

Second-floor plan.

43. Joseph W. Staub House, Indianapolis, Indiana, rear section, 1840-50; front section, c. 1859, James Associates, architects. It is unusual for a house to be added to from the front, but this appears to be the case with the Staub dwelling. The rear kitchen and adjoining bathroom and room C space (see first-floor plan), minus the projecting bay, probably came first, and to this section was added the very formal Renaissance Revival front block, the additional room C space, and the side porch. This construction approximately doubled the space in the 64'3″-deep building. Designed for a town building lot, the house is suitably long and narrow; the side entrance hall and the projecting bay area, however, keep the floor plan from being simply a boring progression of rooms coupled together in railroad fashion.

The combination entrance hood and balcony enlivens the front façade. The trim of the entrance helps to relieve the building's cold formality. Window heads are limestone lintels on the front, but elsewhere the heads are gracefully arched. The single-light sash windows probably date from late in the 1800s, having replaced multi-light sash.

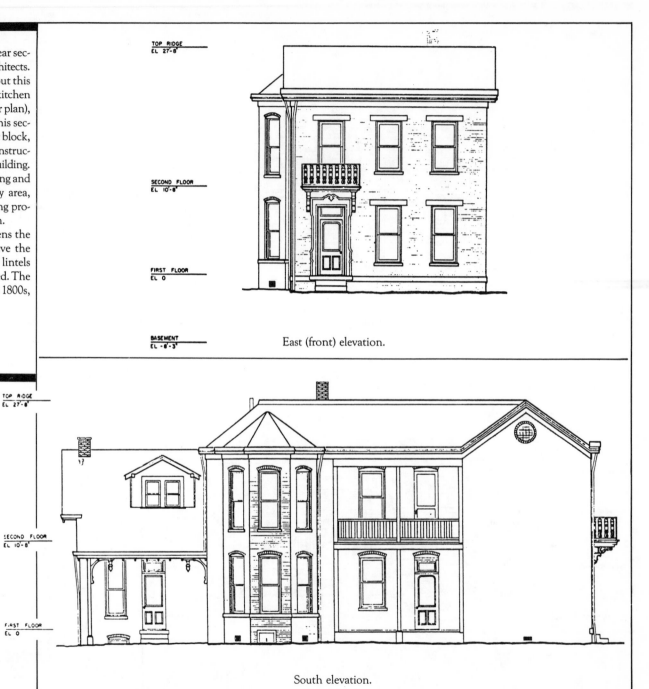

TOP RIDGE
EL 27'-8"

SECOND FLOOR
EL 10'-8"

FIRST FLOOR
EL 0

BASEMENT
EL -8'-3"

East (front) elevation.

TOP RIDGE
EL 27'-8"

SECOND FLOOR
EL 10'-8"

FIRST FLOOR
EL 0

South elevation.

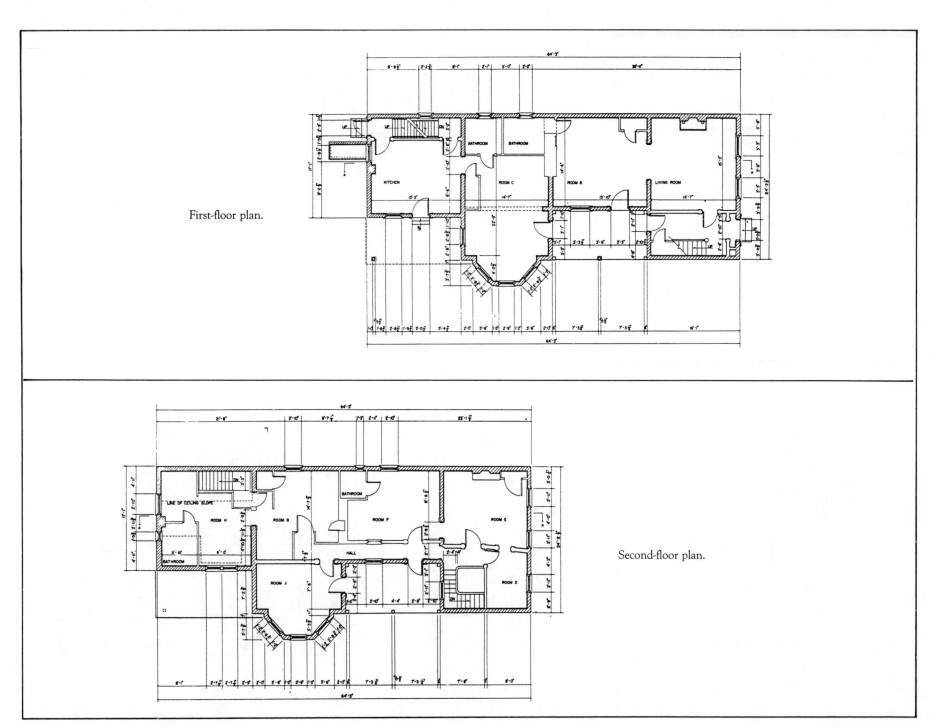

First-floor plan.

Second-floor plan.

44. Robert Matches House, Little Falls, New Jersey, 1854-56, with later side porch addition. The eclectic, coarsed brownstone Matches residence pleasantly combines elements of the Greek Revival, Italianate, and Second Empire styles. The concave mansard roof and handsomely trimmed dormers establish the overall image of Victorian elegance. The main entrance, with its pilasters, side lights and transom, is basically a Greek Revival design; the bracketed cornice and wide roof overhang are exactly those of an Italianate residence. The interior layout allows for six bedrooms, two of which are located on the third floor, spaciously enclosed by the mansard roof. Note on the first-floor plan that the present living room was formerly a double parlor.

Southwest (front) elevation.

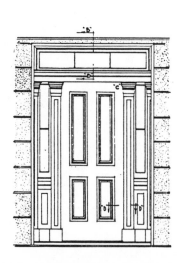

Main entrance elevation, exterior.

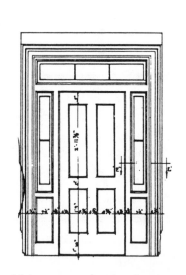

Main entrance elevation, interior.

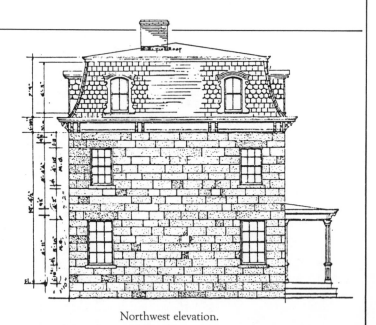

Northwest elevation.

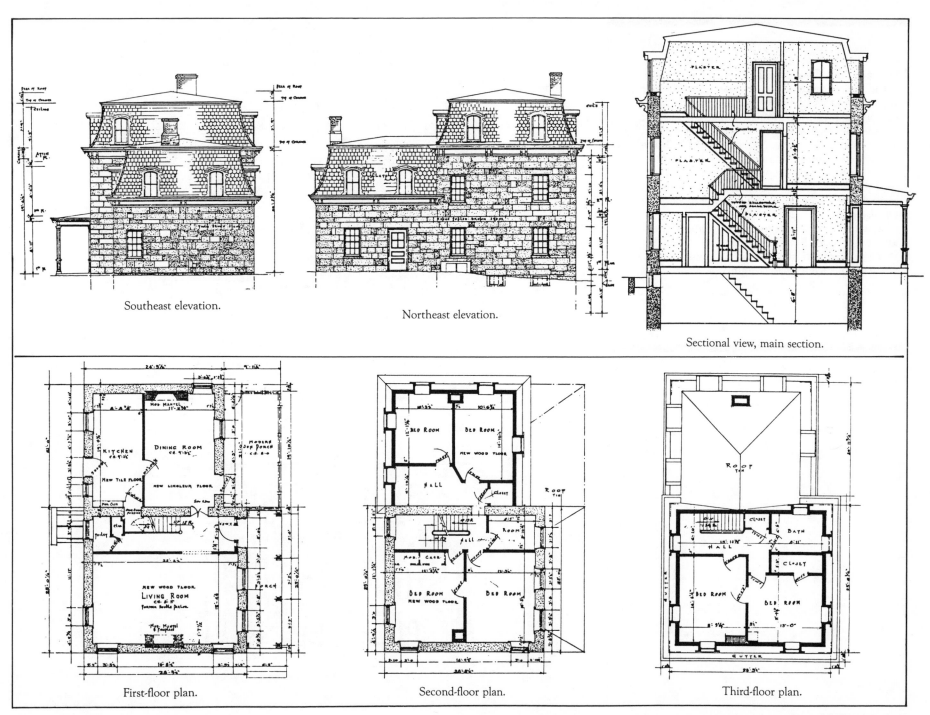

Southeast elevation.

Northeast elevation.

Sectional view, main section.

First-floor plan.

Second-floor plan.

Third-floor plan.

45. **Mrs. S. L. Gant House**, Nebraska City, Nebraska, mid-1800s. As simple and symmetrical as Nebraska farmland, Mrs. Gant's dwelling is a great deal more typical of the domestic architecture in America's heartland than Grant Wood's Gothic Revival farmhouse. What particularly distinguishes the Gant design is the use of a two-story verandah, Greek Revival entrances at both the first- and second-floor levels, and roof cresting. Whoever the carpenter-builder was, he surely knew how to take a simple center-hall Colonial box and give it graceful Victorian touches. The first-floor has almost 11' ceilings, and the front windows are scaled accordingly to allow for the passage of light.

A full-size basement (see floor plan) contains the kitchen, laundry, boiler room, and a bedroom. To allow for better ventilation of this below-ground space, semicircular wells were placed around each window.

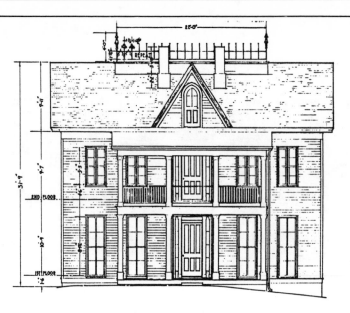

East (front) elevation.

West elevation.

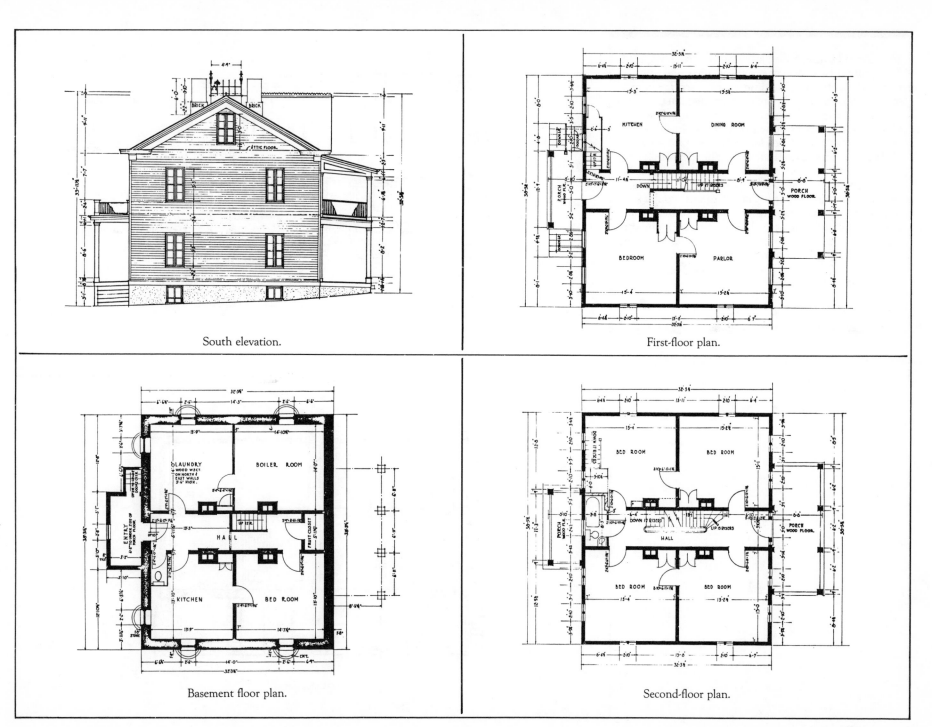

South elevation.

First-floor plan.

Basement floor plan.

Second-floor plan.

46. Clegg House, Valley Junction vicinity, Iowa, 1865. The most unusual form of American Victorian architecture is the octagonal building. It was used for homes, schoolhouses, and public buildings throughout the country during the mid-century. Orson Squire Fowler, a phrenologist and writer, popularized the eight-sided form in *A Home For All; or, The Gravel Wall and Octagon Mode of Building. . .*, first issued in 1848. The builder of the Clegg house closely followed Fowler's suggestions, even using gravel concrete as the basic building material. It might be thought that only pie-shaped rooms would have resulted from buildings in this form, but, rather, a semi-cruciform floor plan emerged. A square parlor and dining room occupy the center space, and pyramid-shaped rooms occupy the front and rear.

South (front) elevation.

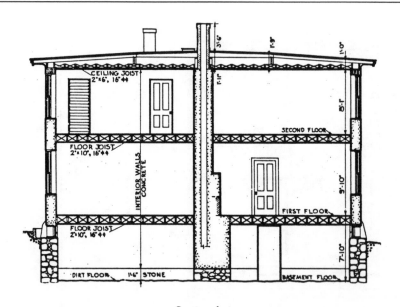

Sectional view.

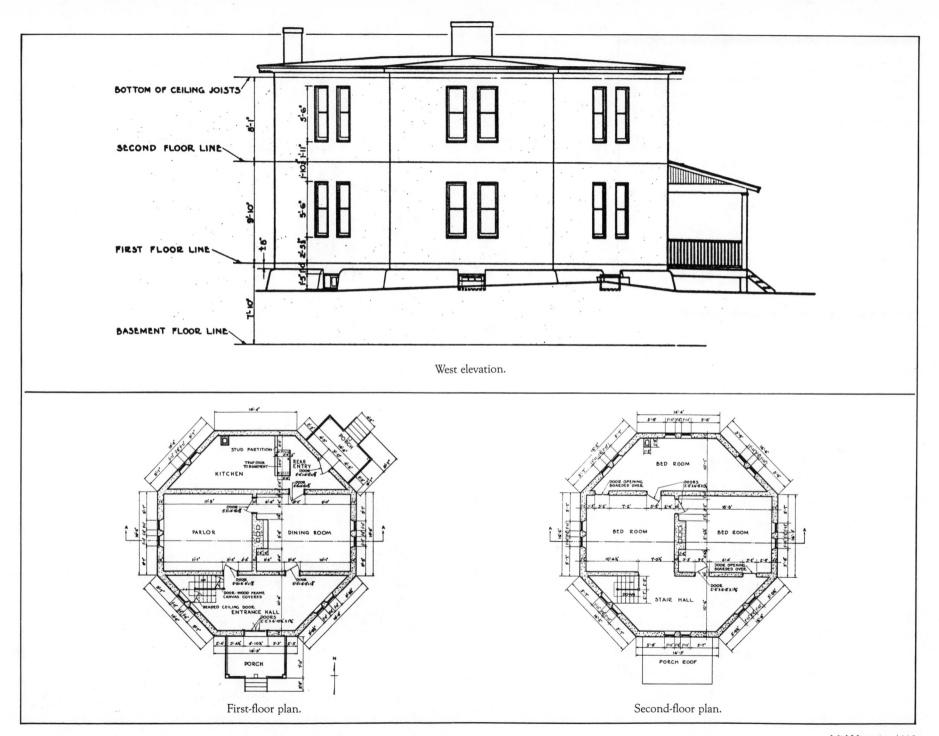

BOTTOM OF CEILING JOISTS

SECOND FLOOR LINE

FIRST FLOOR LINE

BASEMENT FLOOR LINE

West elevation.

STUD PARTITION
TRAP DOOR TO BASEMENT
KITCHEN
REAR ENTRY
DOOR
PORCH
PARLOR
DINING ROOM
DOOR - WOOD FRAME CANVAS COVERED
BEADED CEILING DOOR
ENTRANCE HALL
DOORS
PORCH
N

First-floor plan.

BED ROOM
DOOR OPENING BOARDED OVER
DOORS
BED ROOM
BED ROOM
DOOR
DOOR OPENING BOARDED OVER
STAIR HALL
PORCH ROOF

Second-floor plan.

47. **Octagonal House**, Afton, Minnesota, 1855. With its cupola and board-and-batten siding, the Afton octagonal house presents a more pleasing appearance than the Iowa residence shown on the preceding pages. The cupola or monitor top is an appealing and practical solution to lighting the attic space. The building has been further dressed up with well-framed windows and a Greek Revival entrance. A conventional side wing—containing the kitchen, pantry, workshop, and wood shed—is neatly joined to the main section. For the most part, the rooms in the octagon are irregularly shaped, but all the space is imaginatively used.

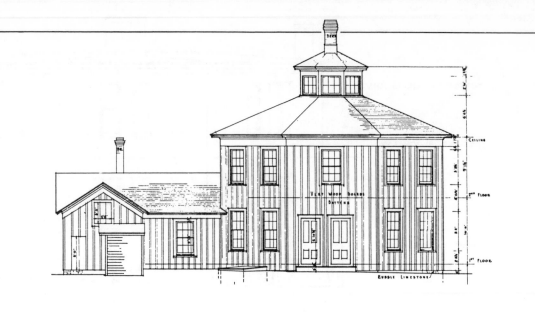

North elevation.

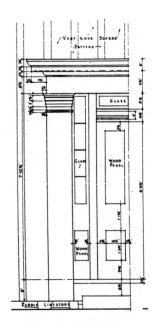

Entrance half-elevation.

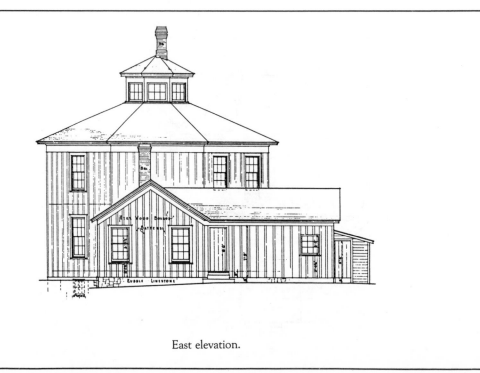

East elevation.

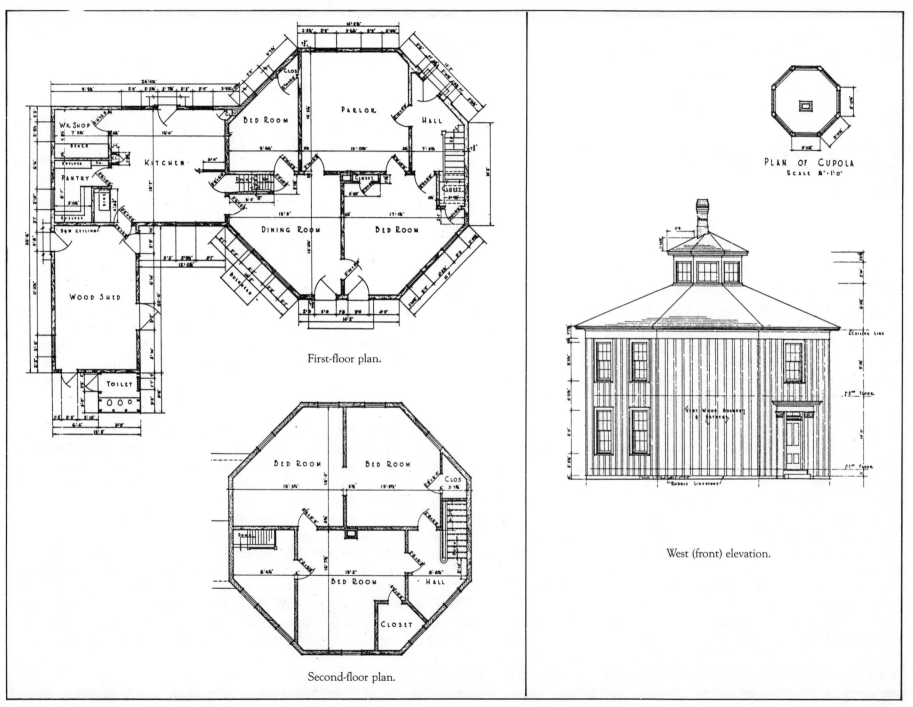

First-floor plan.

Second-floor plan.

PLAN OF CUPOLA
Scale ¼" = 1'·0"

West (front) elevation.

Late Victorian

With the exception of the octagonal house, the various architectural styles in home building introduced by architects and builders in the 1840s and '50s gradually eclipsed the vernacular Colonial in popularity during the post-Civil War decades. Renaissance Revival town houses like the John Eckert House in Madison, Indiana (p. 117), were built in small towns as well as large. Stolid Italianate mansions of the type in which James Whitcomb Riley lived (pp. 118-19) satisfied the most tasteful longings of the upper-middle class from Portland, Maine, to San Francisco. And Second Empire homes with mansard roofs, such as the Sheffield House (pp. 120-21), became even more common in use and elaborate in decoration.

By the mid-1880s, however, all of these forms had been swept aside by a passion for the Queen Anne style. Today considered the most typically "Victorian" in form, Queen Anne houses popped up everywhere—on farms, in villages, on urban boulevards. Not until nearly the end of the century, when the tastemakers began to lead a nostalgic retreat back to the Colonial style, did the ardor for the towering Queen Anne house begin to cool.

Homes such as the modest Chambers-Mayberry House (p. 127) and the fancy William Jennings Bryan Residence (pp. 124-26) were built in the hundreds of thousands for several decades across America and Canada. Always designed with a wide front porch or a wraparound verandah, this type of building—usually wood-frame—has an irregular profile. Gables cross gables and each roof usually has a steep pitch. The main entrance, off a front porch, is almost always positioned off-center. In many homes, such as the Bryan Residence, the entrance is at the base of a tower which also serves as a stair hall. Windows in the main front rooms are likely to be extra large and are often paired or have sidelights.

The picturesque quality of the typical Queen Anne house is emphasized by the use of different building materials—shingles cut in fishscale, diagonal, and rounded patterns; diagonal siding and carved panels; iron cresting and finials; and patterned or colored glass for windows and doors. Smaller Queen Anne houses were built, of course, but the average house appears unusually roomy and intriguing in layout, especially by today's standards. Because of the irregular structure, there is no modern open floor plan or even a traditional center hall, but rather a series of different-sized rooms leading from a front hall or entry. These rooms may extend three or four deep in the larger dwellings, beginning with a front parlor, back parlor or library, dining room, and finally a kitchen with pantry. Because of the use of verandahs, towers, single and double bays, and projecting gables, the rooms are full of interesting angles and corners.

48. John Eckert House, Madison, Indiana, 1872. Among the many fine homes built in this stylish Midwestern community during the mid-1800s is this unusual Renaissance Revival town house. Of only one story, it nevertheless appears to be an imposing structure. The stone and brick construction and the extensive use of metal detailing on the façade give the building a distinct character. Rarely is such exterior ornamentation carried out with such a lavish and skilled hand. Hidden by this fancy front is a string of rooms, opening one into the other, much as the rooms in a "railroad flat". The kitchen is a frame addition with clapboard siding.

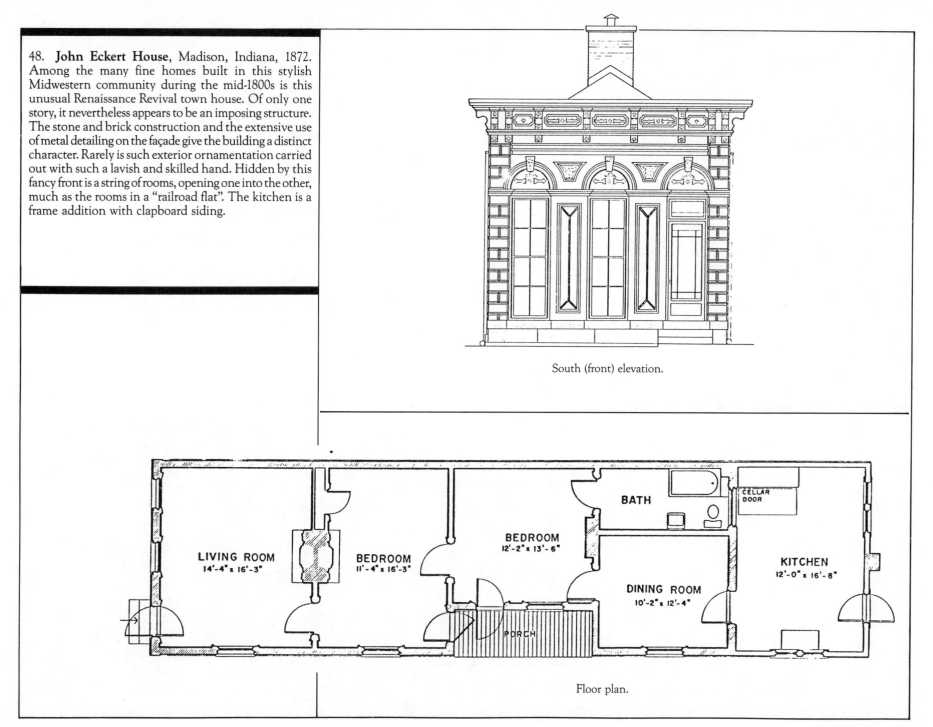

South (front) elevation.

Floor plan.

49. James Whitcomb Riley House, Indianapolis, Indiana, c. 1872. Riley was a longtime guest in the home of John R. Nickum. A spacious Italianate brick mansion, the Nickum house is distinguished by handsomely framed and paired windows, double entrance doors, round-arch window heads on the south (front) façade, and a bracketed and ornamented cornice. The superb balustraded side porch provides a second entrance and leads to the library, probably a place where business was conducted by Nickum or Riley.

The room layout reflects the needs and aspirations of an upper-middle-class family of the late 19th century. The rooms are generously proportioned, and on the first floor are found not parlors but a "library" and a "drawing room." Behind them are two dining rooms, one for formal occasions. All of the rooms for entertaining guests are supplied with fireplaces. The rear wing is for the kitchen and the housekeeper's apartment, a back stairway connecting the two floors. The bedrooms on the second floor, opening on connecting hallways, are also lavishly spaced, with the bedroom in the front even having an adjoining sitting room.

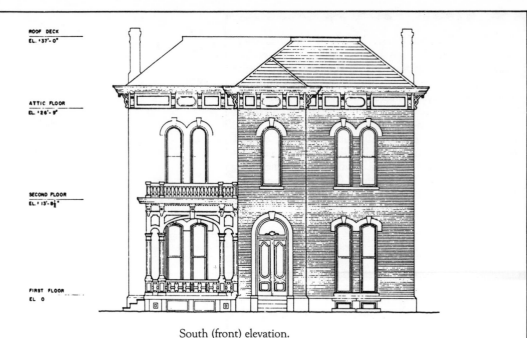

South (front) elevation.

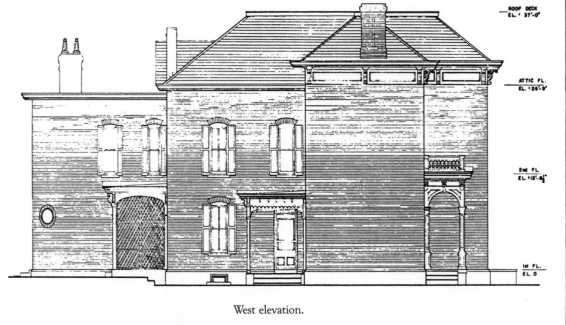

West elevation.

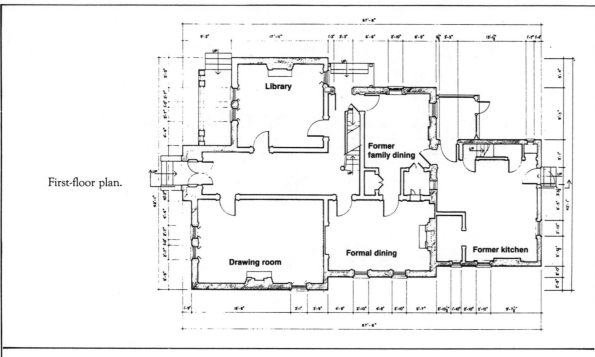

First-floor plan.

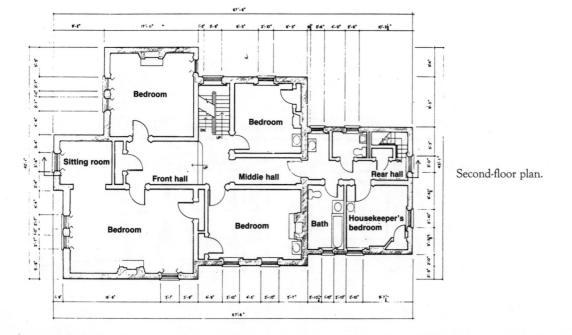

Second-floor plan.

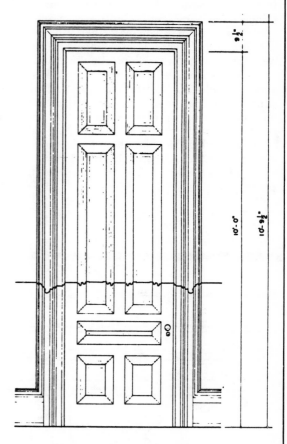

Library and drawing room door elevation.

50. **Sheffield House**, Anaheim, California, late 19th century, Chris Stappenbach, architect. An ideal model for a Second Empire house, the Sheffield residence brings together some of the best elements of Victorian architectural style. The use of a mansard roof—in this case, shingled—makes maximum use of the second-floor space without the building becoming top-heavy in form. Paired window dormers successfully combine pediments and round arches. On the first floor, a double-door entrance and elongated front windows are handsomely set off by a graceful verandah. Spacious, imaginatively designed window bays open up the south side of the house. Tying all four sides of the house together is a decorative bracketed cornice.

The center-hall floor plan allows for four main rooms on each floor. Modern baths have been incorporated off the first-floor service porch and over a second-floor rear porch.

West (front) elevation.

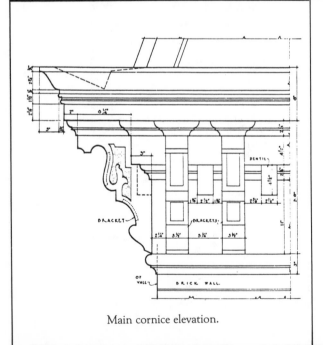

Main cornice elevation.

South elevation.

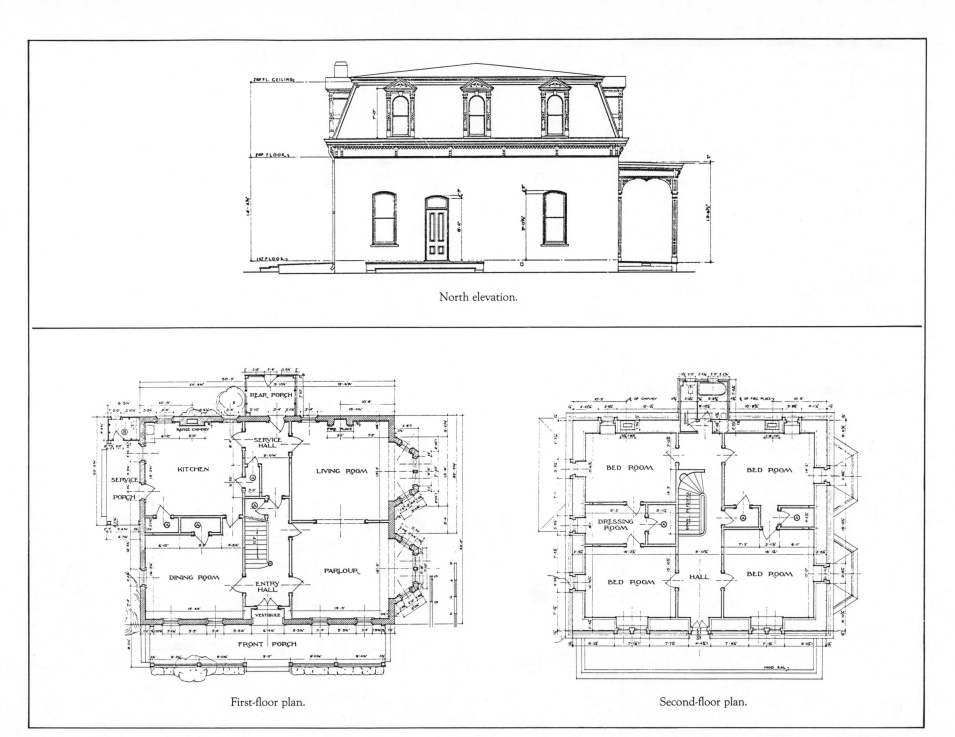

North elevation.

First-floor plan.

Second-floor plan.

51. **Lew M. Meder House**, Carson City, Nevada, late 1870s. This handsome little house displays a decorative charm worthy of imitation today. Few modest 20th-century homes are as carefully and thoughtfully ornamented. The house derives its character from applied corner quoins, square double window bays, an Eastlake entrance, and the double-bracketed cornice which returns at the eaves. Wood has been used throughout, various decorative elements being painted in a color contrasting with the clapboard siding.

The irregular lines allow for an imaginative floor plan, one room being set off from another in a logical but interesting manner. There is more than ample closet space in most of the principal rooms. Only one bedroom was allowed for originally, but a second could be created from the kitchen or front parlor if desired. The floor plan and north and south elevations show a rear addition which might well be used as a new kitchen.

East (front) elevation.

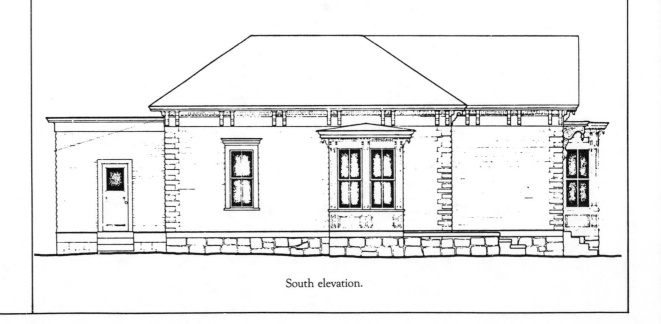

South elevation.

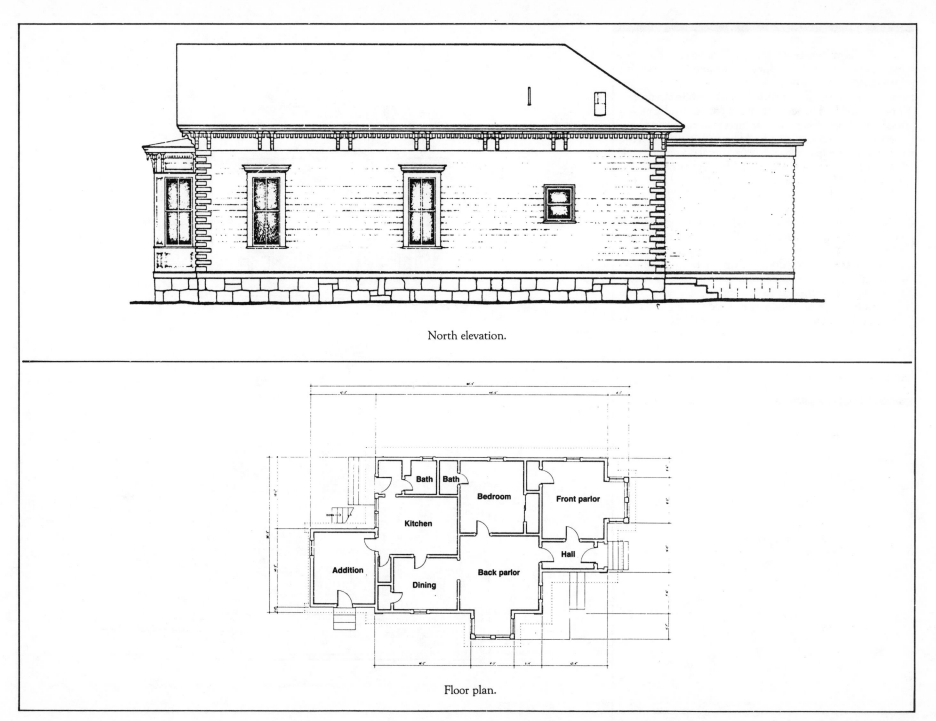

North elevation.

Floor plan.

Bath   Bath

Bedroom

Front parlor

Kitchen

DOWN

Addition

Dining

Back parlor

Hall

52. **William Jennings Bryan Residence**, Lincoln, Nebraska, late 19th century. The famed orator and Democratic candidate for President lived in a most uncommon Queen Anne mansion of more than ten rooms. The soaring hall tower with metal convex and concave roofs and iron cresting is a striking feature of the asymmetrical house design. Double-story window bays on the east and west sides, each with ornamental siding, gracefully open up the house at each end. The decorative paneled and bracketed cornice and wraparound verandah further add to the building's picturesque quality. Only the front entrance seems unduly modest.

The interior room layout and appointments are as lavish as the exterior suggests. The first floor contains a living room, library and sitting room (each connected to the other by sliding doors), a dining room, a pantry, and a kitchen. Fireplaces adorn each of these principal rooms and were included for decorative effect rather than utility. On the second floor are five bedrooms and a large bath. A back stair hall, rising off the kitchen, suggests that the Bryans had live-in household help.

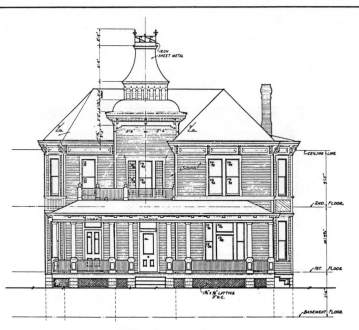

North (front) elevation.

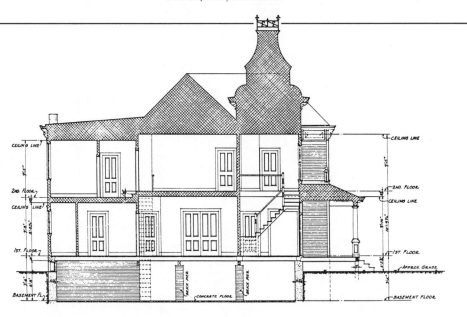

Sectional view.

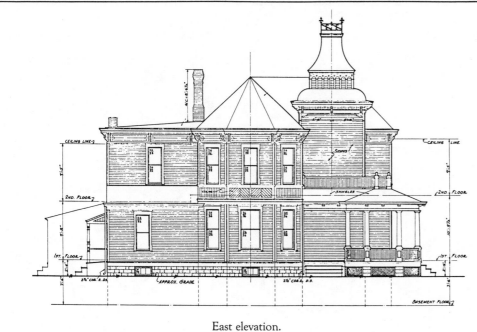

East elevation.

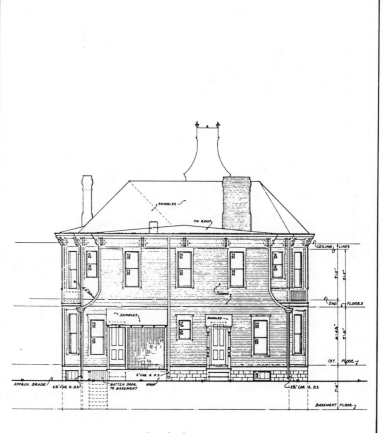

South elevation.

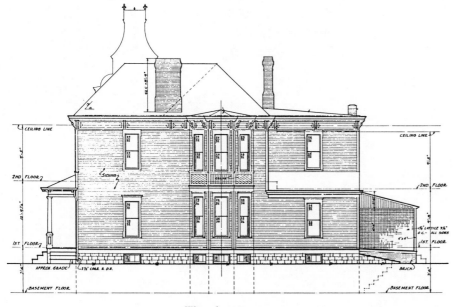

West elevation.

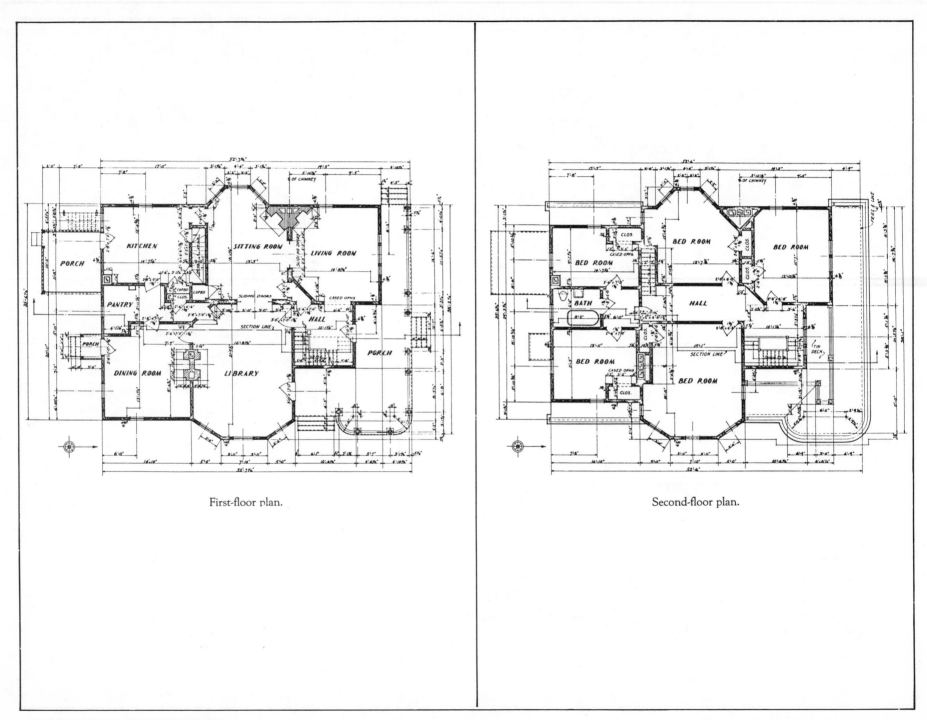

First-floor plan.

Second-floor plan.

53. **Chambers-Mayberry House**, Niobrara, Nebraska, 1909-10, Joseph A. Davis, architect. Although built in the 20th century, the clapboard Queen Anne house has more in common with the Victorian age than the modern. By the time it was sketched, it had lost its decorative cornice, but the decorative tin cresting still remained along the peaks of the hipped roof and dormers. The basic asymmetrical form of the house defines its Victorian character; the lunette window in the gable, and the foursquare entrance, however, suggest the then-growing popularity of Colonial Revival forms. The interior was practically planned with both front and rear stair halls, two baths, a dining room with a built-in china and linen cabinet, and an unusually spacious entry foyer. A corner fireplace adorns the front parlor.

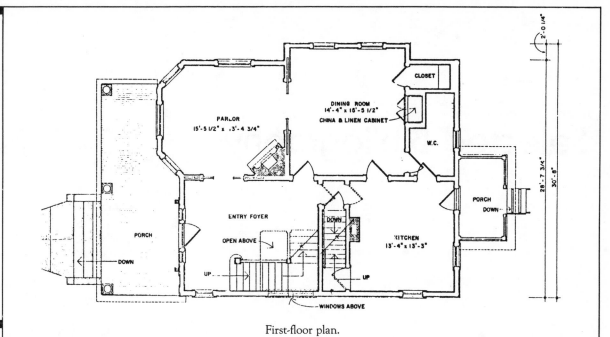

First-floor plan.

East (front) elevation.

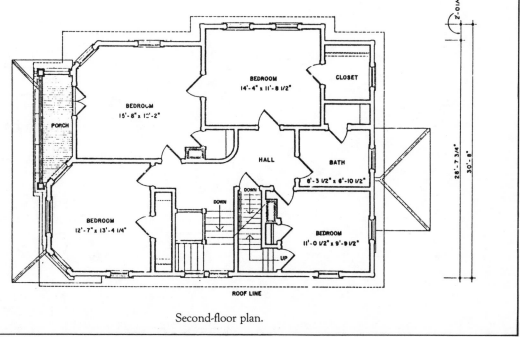

Second-floor plan.

Selected Bibliography

Blumenson, John J.-G. *Identifyng American Architecture: A Pictorial Guide to Styles and Terms, 1600-1945.* Nashville, Tenn.: American Association for State and Local History, 1977.

Cummings, Abbott Lowell. *The Framed Houses of Massachusetts Bay, 1625-1725.* Cambridge Mass.: Harvard University Press, 1979.

Downing, Andrew Jackson. *The Architecture of Country Houses.* Reprint of the 1850 ed. New York: Dover Publications, 1969.

_____. *Cottage Residences.* Reprinted as *Victorian Cottage Residences*, 1873 ed. New York: Dover Publications, 1981.

Grow, Lawrence. *Classic Old House Plans.* Pittstown, N.J.: The Main Street Press, 1984.

_____. *Country Architecture.* Pittstown, N.J.: The Main Street Press, 1985.

Loth, Calder and Julius Trousdale Sadler, Jr. *The Only Proper Style: Gothic Architecture in America.* Boston: New York Graphic Society, 1975.

Poppeliers, John, S. Allen Chambers, Jr., and Nancy B. Schwartz. *What Style Is It? A Guide to American Architecture.* Washington, D.C.: The Preservation Press, 1984.

Rifkind, Carole. *A Field Guide to American Architecture.* New York: New American Library, 1980.

Smith, G.E. Kidder. *The Architecture of the United States.* 3 vols. Garden City, N.Y.: Anchor Press/Doubleday, 1981.

Vaux, Calvert. *Villas and Cottages.* Reprint of the 2nd ed., 1864. New York: Dover Publications, 1970.

Whiffen, Marcus. *American Architecture Since 1780: A Guide to the Styles.* Cambridge, Mass.: The M.I.T. Press, 1969.